A River in Time

The Story of a Peak District River

Christine Gregory

by **Christine Gregory**

A River in Time

The Story of a Peak District River

First published in paperback in 2013 by Grafika Limited
Copyright © Christine Gregory 2013

A catalogue record for this book is available from the British Library
ISBN 978-0-9541089-4-6

Printed and bound in Great Britain

Grafika Limited
Riverside Studio, Riverside Business Park, Buxton Road
Bakewell, Derbyshire DE45 1GS
www.grafika-uk.com

For more information about the Bradford River Action Group
and the River Bradford go to www.riverintime.org.uk

All photographs were taken by the author unless stated otherwise.

Right : River Bradford flowing over a shallow weir at Brookleton

Bradford Dale in early spring

Rivers, springs and wells are places of deep meaning. We use the language of water's flow to describe our feelings. There are depths, shallows; still waters are said to 'run deep'; we can gush, 'well up' with tears, and even drown in our emotions. Bradford Dale is a special place and people's feelings about it run very high. The River Bradford, despite its diminutive size, has a remarkable history. This book aims to draw a picture of the evolution of the river, the surrounding landscape and the people that live close by.

I lived with my family at Coldwell End in a lead miner's cottage where, earlier in the twentieth century, a family of ten had lived with just one bedroom. Our house overlooked Bradford Dale and our garden was in it. For twenty years the dale was the backdrop to my life and I have spent many hours and days exploring the dale and its surrounding hills, woods, lanes and fields. I know this place intimately, but it is a place of contrasts, deep shadows, dazzling light and many surprises. Walking along the River Bradford, the dale is experienced differently with each turn, twist or offshoot of the gorge, the enclosed spaces forcing us to walk in and through the landscape rather than over and across it. This is a place in which past and present are fused in the formation of rocks, river and valley. There are features in this landscape – deep clefts, sudden cliffs, crags and caves – that surprise, even if the forms and paths are familiar. This complex and ever-changing landscape challenges our sense of space, scale and distance and also of time.

Christine Gregory

Contents

Above left to right : Male tufted duck, marsh marigold, grey heron, mallard ducklings, mute swans, field scabious

Left : Red campion on the edge of a dam

Right : Packhorse bridge, the Coach Road

Foreword

by the Rt Hon Lord Smith of Finsbury, Chairman of the Environment Agency

The streams and dales and landscapes of the White Peak are amongst the most beautiful we have, and I have spent many a happy day walking through this land, contemplating the beauty of the natural world, the richness of its biodiversity, and the refreshment that it can bring to the human spirit. This is especially true of the River Bradford, which has flowed through time, beauty and the lives of its people for centuries. Running streams are vital to us, not only for sustenance, for the provision of essential support to our human existence, nor just for the support they afford to an astonishing variety of natural life, but for the way they calm us, and move us, and provide us with a glimpse of something more profound than our everyday world.

This book tells us about all of this, and more, in relation to the River Bradford. It tells us about its history, about the communities it sustains, and about the natural biodiversity it supports. It gives us the next best thing to walking along its banks and hearing it run. And it helps us to understand that better, when we do.

It also, however, and rightly, identifies the threats the river faces – indeed, the threats we all face for the future of our human life on this fragile earth. Two years ago, the River Bradford dried up. The severe drought that brought this about was part of an increasing pattern of extreme weather that is now affecting us, and many other parts of the world. In recent years we have experienced serious droughts and serious floods, sometimes in very rapid succession. The rivers we are used to can become a trickle or turn into a raging and destructive torrent. And the science of climate change tells us that we are going to see more extremes of weather, more unpredictability, more floods and more droughts, as the impact of our greenhouse gases on the earth's atmosphere continues to increase.

That is why conserving water, striving to protect glorious rivers like the Bradford, and nurturing our delicate ecosystems, become so important. *A River in Time* tells us why the River Bradford is so vital to us all. But in doing so, it tells us wider truths, too, about the huge importance of the whole of our natural world.

Chris Smith
August 2013

Introduction

The River Bradford has a central place in the life and character of the local communities of Middleton, Youlgrave and Alport. Visitors and local people enjoy the dale throughout the year and value this unique example of the Derbyshire Dales landscape. The combination of wildness and accessibility draws many here who feel a strong connection to this place. People walk the dale throughout the year to exercise themselves and their dogs or to quietly contemplate the river and the creatures that live in it. Bradford Dale and the river itself may be small in scale but they are home to a wide range of flora and fauna. Along the river there are unvisited places that are havens for wildlife and rare plants. Throughout Bradford Dale there are delicate ecosystems that depend on the general health of the river and of the dale itself.

The appearance of the dale has been altered down the years by agriculture and industry. Bradford Dale was once a working place with a sheep dip, corn mill, factory and wheelwright's shop. Lead miners passed through the dale on their way to the lead rakes and some even mined in the dale. In the past people walked the dale not for pleasure but for work, but the signs of past industry are mostly obscured by the encroachment of trees and ground cover. The landscape around the River Bradford and the river itself were shaped by people for various uses in the past, and human activity continues to influence the flow and ecology of the river for both good and ill.

Left : Brookleton, Youlgrave

Great concern has been focussed recently on the future supply and demand for water both nationally and globally, and the community of Youlgrave faced its own crisis when the cherished River Bradford ceased to flow from August until December 2011. This mirrored a countrywide problem of drought and loss of flow in rivers at that time. As a consequence of the drought, a public meeting was held in Youlgrave in October 2011 and was attended by around 150 people. This sparked off a local discussion about weather, climate change, local water use and the possibilities of protecting the river from drying up. A group of local people decided to carry on meeting and to find out more about the flow of the river, to establish where it was leaking and to consider what could be done to conserve its future health. The Bradford River Action Group (BRAG) was formed and it was decided that the unique history and ecology of this little limestone river should be explored further and celebrated. This book, funded by the Peak District National Park Sustainable Development Fund, is a result.

Following the drought of 2011, 2012 saw record rainfall across Britain, with widespread flooding and the disruption of homes, transport and agriculture. The rivers of the Derbyshire Dales were swollen, the fields sodden and the water table at its highest in years. Extreme weather as a result of climate change, and dire warnings about the future, force us to face our relationship to the natural environment. Water is the source of all life on the planet and yet it also has immense destructive power.

The first part of the book, **The Making of the Derbyshire Dales Landscape**, outlines some of the geological processes that formed the River Bradford and the Derbyshire Dales. A fuller account of the evolution of the landscape of the Peak District is provided in Appendix 1. Part 1 then looks at key phases of human settlement in the surrounding area and the impact on the landscape and rivers made by the monastic grange farms, enclosures and lead mining.

Part 2: **A Journey along the River and through the Past** is a kind of mini-travelogue along the river, from its source to the confluence with the River Lathkill. It explores evidence of previous uses of the river, noting where the monastic grange farms were located and where the ancient trackways and trade routes passed close by the river or crossed over it. As the journey progresses, flora and fauna that can be seen along different stretches of the river are pictured, together with explanations of how certain creatures and plants exploit the varied habitats that the dale and waterside offer.

Middleton and Youlgrave depended on the river for their water and for industry. These communities' connection to the river is an important part of the river's story and is explored in this part of the book. The journey ends at Alport, once a major centre for both mining and smelting lead.

Lead is at the heart of any story of the White Peak and its people, and also of its rivers, and so Part 3: **The Impact of Lead Mining** is entirely focussed on the industry and the extraordinary efforts made to 'unwater' the mines of Alport, which have had a major impact on the hydrology of the whole area.

Modifications made to the flow, levels and direction of the river have 'ravelled it up' over time. In Part 4: **Restoring the River,** Warren Slaney, Head River Keeper for the Haddon Estate, outlines his project of 'unravelling' the river and taking it back on its natural course. Warren discusses the conflicts inherent in managing a river that attracts crowds of visitors, many of whom are unaware of the effect they have on the river and its wildlife.

Part 5: **The Future** reflects on recent extremes of drought and flood and considers how some of the projections made by climate scientists could have an impact on this river and landscape. The story of collapsing soughs (drainage channels made by lead miners) is central to any consideration of the river's future and is a recurring theme in the book. Members of Youlgrave Waterworks describe the challenges they face in continuing to supply water to the residents of Youlgrave.

Throughout the book, local residents share memories of their river and its dale that go back well before the motorcar brought thousands of visitors to the place.

The River Bradford can be viewed as a microcosm, a lens through which the larger picture of human relationship to rivers, the land and our fellow creatures can be seen a little more clearly. When a river dries up, it sends a message that we know, at the deepest levels of our conscious and unconscious minds, 'all is not well'. The sound of running water connects us to the most basic functions of our life-sustaining world. We cannot live without water. When water ceases to flow, we are forced to ask, 'What now? What next?'

This book is a celebration and a reflection on what a precious thing a river is; uniting past, present and future as it flows from source to confluence in a cycle of endless change and renewal.

July 2013

Left : Grey wagtail with water crowfoot **Right** : Coot family
Far right : The River Bradford laced with water crowfoot flowering in June

Part 1

The Making of the Derbyshire Dales Landscape

'The water is more productive than the earth. Nay, the earth hath no fruitfulness without showers or dews; for all the herbs, and flowers, and fruit, are produced and thrive by the water; and the very minerals are fed by streams that run under ground, whose natural course carries them to the tops of many high mountains, as we see by several springs breaking forth on the tops of the highest hills; and this is also witnessed by the daily trial and testimony of several miners.'

Isaac Walton, *The Compleat Angler*, 1653

View across Bradford Dale to Harthill Castle Ring and Robin Hood's Stride

The Making and Breaking of Rocks by Water

Looking across the open fields and rolling hills of the White Peak, all is not as it first appears. The limestone plateau is in fact cut through by deep, unseen dales and gorges that give a visual lie to the apparent 'lie of the land', in this open, pastoral landscape. Viewed from a distance there is little indication of the hidden worlds contained within the dales and gorges. The formation of this landscape is the result of great climatic and geological events. In essence the story is about the making and breaking of rocks by water.

The view westwards across the south-east corner of the limestone plateau

Bradford Dale and its river were sculpted by the formative processes of the deep past. The bony rock outcrops that dominate the skyline at Moatlow Knob, the steep slopes, small caves, rock shelters and bubbling springs are typical of the landscape features of the Derbyshire Dales.

There is a fuller account of the complex geological processes that made this landscape in Appendix 1. Readers who wish to understand more about what shaped the dales, the composition of rocks and minerals, and the flow of rivers and underground drainage systems, should refer to this for a more detailed understanding of the landscape and hydrology of the area.

The limestone of the Derbyshire Dales is made from the remains of sea creatures that formed layers of sediment on the floor of a shallow tropical sea between 360 and 310 million years ago. There were reefs (built up from algae, not coral) around the edges of this sea, rather like a Pacific atoll of today. Throughout the period in which the sediments were settling and limestone forming, sporadic eruptions of volcanoes spewed lava across the shallow sea bed, which, when hardened, formed layers of basalt across the limestone. The layers of basalt are known locally as 'toadstone' (due to their green/brown spotted appearance). Volcanic ash settled over the water or onto exposed stone to form layers of what is called 'tuff'. These layers of volcanic rock – toadstones – have been important for both miners and farmers in helping them detect springs and lead veins, as the relatively impermeable lavas and the ash deposits restrict vertical water movement and give rise to spring lines along their top surface where they crop out on valley sides.

The younger rocks of the Dark Peak (the Millstone Grit) were made from sediments that washed down through a gigantic river delta from mountains that were being eroded far to the north. The limestone lay buried under these younger sedimentary rocks for millennia until seismic forces (over millions of years) raised the Derbyshire Dome, which it is thought was once 3,000 metres high. The mountains were worn away over time eventually to reveal the limestone, the oldest rock of the Peak District.

This limestone outcrop extends to over 500 square kilometres between Castleton in the north and Wirksworth in the south. The topography of the White Peak and of the Yorkshire Dales is referred to by geologists as 'karst', and is largely shaped by the dissolving action of water on limestone. Features typical of karst topography are sinkholes, vertical shafts, disappearing streams, springs and caves. This Swiss cheese-like formation has developed over a long period of geological time.

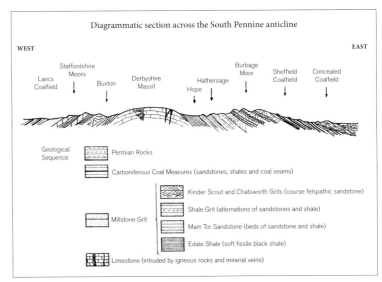

Diagram by Dr Trevor D. Ford

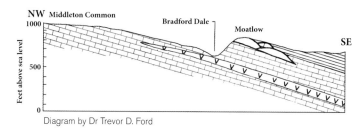

Diagram by Dr Trevor D. Ford

There are three types of limestone, each associated with different landforms. The White Peak's central plateau has the shallow 'shelf' limestone which was deposited in a lagoon. This is characterised by a soft undulating landscape. In the south-west of the White Peak are the deeper 'basin' limestones. Around the edges of the central shelf are 'reef' limestones characterised by hard weather-resistant conical hills such as Thorpe Cloud, Wetton Hill and Chrome and Parkhouse Hills (close to Earl Sterndale), all known as 'reef knolls'. The reef forms were built up from mounds of sediment that were then further colonised by other marine creatures. There are other examples of reef limestone close to the River Bradford in the Moatlow outcrop above Bradford Dale, Raenstor (or Rhienstor) near Alport *(see page 69)* and in the sheer rock face above Rowlow Brook opposite Smerrill Grange Farm near Middleton-by-Youlgrave.

Over the last two million years variations in climate have caused successive ice ages when glaciers formed and advanced, interspersed by warmer periods known as interglacials when the edges of the glaciers retreated. Great volumes of melt water from thawing snowfields shaped the current valleys of the Derbyshire Dales. It is uncertain where the early river systems of the Peak District were, but it seems likely that they flowed in an easterly direction. As the ice retreated, boulders, powdered rocks and melt-water scoured steep-sided gorges through the limestone. As these volumes of water no longer flow, there are many dry valleys in the White Peak and rivers that flow underground in drier seasons.

The geology and hydrology of this area have made a unique landscape that has, in turn, shaped the lives and fortunes of those that live here.

The pastures of the limestone plateau are valuable grazing land. Its soils are composed of 'loess' – windblown silts deposited during the last ice age when much of the Peak District was high, freezing tundra. This rich loam has sustained farming activity over millennia. In higher, more exposed areas such as the land above and on the sides of Gratton Dale and Lathkill Dale, there is rough pasture and relict limestone heath.

Bradford Dale is on the south-eastern corner of the limestone plateau, at the edge of a downward arched fold (or syncline) in the limestone, which extends beneath shales and gritstone to the south-east. What makes the landscape especially rich around the River Bradford is the close proximity of the different kinds of bedrock. A walk up the hill to Mawstone or Robin Hood's Stride (a gritstone tor) will take you across limestone, shales and gritstone with their very different associated flora and fauna. There are different worlds within just a few paces of each other.

View from Youlgrave across Bradford Dale to Harthill Castle Ring and Robin Hood's Stride

The four remaining stones of Nine Stones Close and Robin Hood's Stride

Human Settlement in and around Bradford Dale

Over many hundreds of years places of meaning, habitation, agriculture, trade and worship were linked through ancient routes, and it is easy to picture those that walked here before us. Neolithic then Bronze Age people made clearings in the forests and began the enterprise of farming, and later the Abbeys set to work on exploiting the wild uplands by setting their sheep on them. They planted crops on the richer soils and cultivated hay meadows. They produced food from the rivers, with fish pools and cress beds for winter greens.

There is evidence of human settlement close to Bradford Dale from the Bronze Age and earlier. There are stone circles on all sides of Youlgrave. There is the Neolithic henge monument, Arbor Low, to the west; the Bronze Age Nine Ladies on Stanton Moor; and Nine Stones Close to the south-east of the village, near the gritstone outcrop of Robin Hood's Stride, which itself bears marks and signs of early human presence. Above Bradford Dale, on the southern skyline, the Iron Age settlement at Harthill Moor Farm is clearly evident as a raised plateau alongside Robin Hood's Stride.[1]

An ancient trackway, the Portway, links Iron Age forts and earlier sites of worship along a south-east to north-west route that connects (among many other ancient sites) Mam Tor, Fin Cop, Harthill Castle Ring and Nine Stones Close. It then proceeds on southwards to Wirksworth. According to Dodd and Dodd in *Peakland Roads and Trackways*, the Anglo-Saxon invaders gave the name of the Portway to parts of routes through the Peak District that had been used by travellers from prehistoric times:

'We may assume that the trackway would pass close to the Harthill Moor Stone Circle … and we may further assume that, during the Iron Age, the hillfort known as Castle Ring … was constructed to dominate this length of the trackway. We are in an area that was populous a thousand years before the Iron Age people threw up Castle Ring.'

This ancient trade and communication route would have given access to this otherwise remote area and helped to establish early societies.

Numerous finds of flint and chert tools, jewellery and stone vessels have provided proof of Neolithic and Bronze Age burial, ritual, hunting and of agriculture.

The Victorian archaeologist and local landowner Thomas Bateman excavated many of the Bronze Age burial mounds that were to be found on almost every hilltop or 'low' in the area.[2] His finds were supplemented by many discoveries made by local farmers when working the land. The area is littered with tumuli or barrows, which indicate a relatively dense population of early Britons. Clearly this area was held to be valuable as a place both to live and worship from the earliest times.

There were other reasons to value this area. The mineral wealth of the Derbyshire Dales was discovered by the Romans, who were the first to find, mine and smelt lead here. Lead pigs (ingots of lead metal) with Latin writing engraved on them were found near Matlock and there is evidence of Roman presence in Smerrill, in the form of Romano-British pottery, which was discovered there in 1844.

There are signs of Anglo-Saxon settlement in and around Youlgrave: a Saxon Cross was removed from the centre of the village in the nineteenth century and now stands in the churchyard; an Anglo-Saxon bead has been found at Mawstone, just south of Youlgrave.[3] All Saints Parish Church was built around 1130, but may have had Saxon origins. However it is the proximity of the Portway to Youlgrave that indicates the presence and passage of people over thousands of years.

[1] Robin Hood's Stride has been called 'Mock Beggars' Hall' in the past as its profile against the skyline has the appearance of an ancient building with two great chimneys.
[2] 'Low' means mound or hill and many of the limestone plateau lows are ancient burial mounds. [3] PDNP *Youlgrave Conservation Area Appraisal*, 2010, p6.

Smerrill Grange Farm and 'Fishpond Dale' in winter

The Middle Ages

Derbyshire was in the Saxon kingdom of Mercia and during the reign of Edward the Confessor the Manor of Youlgrave belonged to a Saxon landowner named Colle. After the Norman invasion, William the Conqueror handed out huge parcels of land as reward to his most favoured Earls. One William de Ferrars received *'nearly a hundred manors in this county'* and included among them was the manor of *Giolgrave* (one of the very many names for Youlgrave). *Giolgrave* is noted in the Domesday survey as having *'three ox-gangs of land for geld, three ploughs and land for three ploughs, one villein and one plough, one mill and four acres of meadow'*. The presence of a corn mill in the survey shows that arable crops were cultivated at that time. De Ferrars also received the chapelries of Harthill, Birchover, Stanton, Elton and Winster, the townships of Birchover, Gratton and Middleton and the hamlets of Smerrill, Conksbury, Hartlemoor, Alport and Greenfield. He later gained the title of Earl of Derby, as reward for valour in a battle against the Scots at North Allerton. William de Ferrars was later seized for insurrection and his lands passed to William Peverel, who is said to be the illegitimate son of William the Conqueror.

In 1102 the Norman family of the Peverels granted Haddon to the Knight Avenal who appears as the first owner of Haddon Hall in the estate records. One of his successors gave Meadow Place and Conksbury to the Abbey of Leicester in 1220. Much of the land in and around Youlgrave was retained by the Abbey of Leicester (an Augustinian Order) until the Dissolution of the Monasteries in the 1530s.

There was a medieval settlement at Smerrill, about a mile south-east of Middleton and a short distance from Smerrill Grange, a monastic grange farm situated high above a dale through which the River Bradford runs and where the farm still bears that name *(see pages 22-23)*.

The medieval village of Conksbury, or *Cranchesbury* as it was named in the Domesday Book, takes its name from cranes that may once have lived in the water meadows there. According to the Lichfield Archives,

twenty-eight householders paid Easter Tithes in 1348 and yet there is no trace of this village or Smerrill in later records. It is possible that their disappearance may be accounted for by the Plague pandemic that swept through Europe. The Black Death was at its height in the year 1349 and killed a third to a half of the population of Britain. Many communities were devastated by the Plague but there were also land and people clearances associated with the establishment of the monastic granges in the thirteenth and fourteenth centuries that cannot be discounted when considering the fate of these medieval villages.

Monastic Grange Farms

There has been farming activity in the White Peak from prehistoric times. Ancient agricultural tools worked by Bronze Age farmers have been found by their successors over the last few hundred years. Remains of their places of worship and burial are evident throughout the limestone plateau in numerous stone circles and burial mounds (tumuli). However, taming the landscape and exploiting its pastures for grazing sheep and cultivating crops was the major enterprise of the monasteries, which managed the land and developed new techniques in farming throughout the Middle Ages until the Dissolution in the 1530s.

In the Middle Ages monasteries owned a great deal of land throughout England. Land was given to them, often in remote areas, by landowners hoping to secure a place in heaven and a more secure social standing on this earth.

[4] R.W. Southern, *Western Society and the Church in the Middle Ages*, p245. [5] ibid., p256. [6] There are different theories about the date of the last wolves in England. *'In the fourteenth century wolves were allegedly numerous in areas such as the forests of the Derbyshire Peak'*. Dr Derek Yalden (President of the Mammal Society) thought this unlikely. Some experts believe they may have been exterminated as early as 1300. Successive monarchs were set on their destruction and they were certainly extinct in England and Wales by the end of the fifteenth century, but lingered on in the Highlands of Scotland until around 1700. R. Lovegrove, *Silent Fields*, p21.

'The social upheavals of the eleventh century had brought into secure positions in the feudal structure many new families, of modest means but with the instincts of great landlords. They wanted that symbol of territorial stability – a religious house where they would be honoured as founders and patrons, and buried with decency in the midst of their families.' [4]

Sometimes the land was let to tenants but increasingly the monks and nuns took direct control of land to manage it for profit. The growing market for wool, lead and foodstuffs meant that well-managed land could render a large income. As part of the feudal system and as owners of the manors, religious orders could exploit free labour from poor villagers. The Cistercian Order, whose pioneering methods of land management were gradually adopted by other religious orders, operated a different system. They established satellite monastic grange farms that were worked by laymen under strict monastic discipline as lay brothers. The expansion of the Order and the growth of its worldly success was dramatic and can be explained by the rigorous control they exerted over every aspect of religious, managerial, commercial and farming life. It seems that every detail of grange management was considered. For example: *'Pig-styes can be two or even three leagues from a grange, but pigs, though they can wander by day, must return to the styes at night. Swine herds and shepherds must get their daily food from their abbey or grange.'* [5]

The Cistercians exploited the marginal, undeveloped lands away from the settled areas of Europe and they became the great sheep farmers of England. They were a pioneer force, intent on colonising the wilds of such upland areas as the Peak District. The extensive limestone heath and coarse vegetation of the uplands was fit only for sheep, the wool and meat of which were immensely valuable to the economy of the times. Pack-horses would have taken the wool from the remote areas of the White Peak along the ancient trackways and trading routes that existed at this time. Some wool would be taken along routes that led east towards the Humber for shipping to Europe. At this time English wool was a major export and great profits were made from this and from other surplus products (such as corn or meat). The abbeys were also able to fill their coffers with profits from

lead mining on the land they had been given. All of this wealth was fed back to the monasteries, which became extremely rich.

The monastic systems of land management, animal husbandry and increased production laid the foundations of what we understand as farming and led to the taming of the wilderness that much of Britain once was. The upland landscape of the Peak District was wild indeed, and many believed that wolves roamed the remote and dense forests of the Derbyshire Peak well into the fourteenth century.[6]

Daniel Defoe, who travelled through the Peak District on horseback in the early eighteenth century, described it as a *'howling wilderness'* and *'the most desolate, wild and abandoned country in Great Britain'*.

While the wealth of the monastic grange farms was generated for the mother abbey, it was also important to the food economy, care and well-being of medieval communities. The monasteries were centres for agriculture, manufacture, food production and education, as well as for religious worship.

However, the influence of the monastic granges (as distinct from the monasteries) was not always benevolent, as the principal goal of generating wealth for the abbey was sometimes in conflict with the interests of local inhabitants and on occasion led to land clearances. This might well have been the fate of the villages of Conksbury and Smerrill.

There were several monastic granges located close by the River Bradford and the River Lathkill. The major monastic settlement and the largest of the granges in the area was Meadow Place Grange, *Medoc Plec,* which lay above Lathkill Dale, due north of Youlgrave towards Over Haddon. It was owned and controlled by the Abbey of Leicester along with much of the land in the area and the lead mines at *Medoc Plec.* Roystone Grange, the most well-researched and documented of all the monastic granges in the White Peak, is typical of the Cistercian granges, and lies about six miles south of Youlgrave. Smerrill Grange, another large establishment (order unknown), was located between Elton and Middleton-by-Youlgrave. Mouldridge Grange (Augustinian) near Pikehall was at the southern end of Gratton Dale. There were other, smaller monastic granges including One Ash Grange (Cistercian) above Lathkill Dale, and various writers have surmised that monastic settlements may have existed in Middleton itself and at Alport, where Monks Hall possibly had its origins as a grange.

'Mere' or dewpond at Kenslow

Water Supply

The settlement and fortunes of people across the globe rest on the ability of communities to find and exploit water supplies. As far as water supply is concerned, the limestone uplands of the White Peak have presented a challenge to its people from the earliest times.

In the White Peak, rivers can run dry in the summer and surface water disappears underground, so farmers had to know where springs rose or where wells and boreholes could be sunk. This is still the case in sheep and cattle country and water supply to farms in times of drought continues to present a problem. Nearly all the farms now have licenses to take or 'abstract' ground water from boreholes. This practice has been contentious in times of drought when groundwater levels have become very low with consequent loss of river flows.

Farmers have, in the past, relied on dewponds (or what are locally called 'meres') to provide water for their stock on the high pastures and the dry places of the plateau dotted with farms and small farming hamlets. But this landscape could not sustain whole settlements. Larger communities formed instead on the edges of the plateau along the river courses and dale sides. The villages of Youlgrave and Middleton-by-Youlgrave owe their very existence to the precious flow of the River Bradford. And it is the exploitation of the river for domestic consumption, for fishing, industry, mining and agriculture over centuries that has shaped the watercourse that exists now.

Enclosure of the Commons

Above the dales, the dominant feature of the limestone pastures is the dry-stone walls. These help to define the landscape, giving it distinctive field patterns that have shaped the character of the White Peak. It is likely that the very first farmers built stone enclosures and certainly the grange farms encroached on the open land of the moors by building walls to manage their flocks. Enclosure of the commons of England began in the Middle Ages, with ensuing loss of the open field system and cultivation of arable crops. As sheep farming was highly profitable and not labour-intensive,

it often replaced subsistence farming with consequent depopulation of rural areas.

The landscape that we see today largely has its origins in the main period of enclosure of pastures which occurred in the eighteenth and early nineteenth centuries, when common grazing land was allocated to landowners by Act of Parliament between the 1750s and 1860s. It was then that the enclosure of upland moors and the lower commons close to habitation fundamentally altered the appearance and use of the land in the White Peak.

The Bradford Dale area was enclosed quite late on and it was not until the Youlgrave and Middleton Enclosure Award of 1818 that most of the common land surrounding the village was allocated to large landowners: the Duke of Devonshire, the Duke of Rutland, and Thomas Bateman of Middleton-by-Youlgrave. The losses to the people of Youlgrave and Middleton are evident in the 1799 Manor Survey Map of Youlgrave depicting the 'Mootlowe Common' and 'Coldwell End Common' which had been the villagers' commons along Bradford Dale. For the poorest people unable to hold or to rent a parcel of land, the loss of commons throughout Britain from the Middle Ages onwards meant the loss of grazing and the right to collect firewood and cut peat or turf (turbary). These rights were the basis of subsistence for the rural poor and their loss is what drove many people off the land and into the 'dark satanic mills' of the emerging industries of the industrial revolution.

'In agriculture the years between 1760 and 1820 are the years of wholesale enclosure in which, in village after village, common rights are lost and the landless … labourer is left to support the tenant farmer, the landowner and the tithes of the church.' E. P. Thompson, *The Making of the English Working Class*, 1963.

The law locks up the man or woman
Who steals the goose from off the common
But lets the greater felon loose
Who steals the common from off the goose

Anonymous protest poem from the seventeenth century.

Above : Drystone walls near Kenslow **Below** : Manor Survey Map of 'Youlgrave, 1799' (reproduced with permission of Haddon Estate)

Lead Mining and Quarrying

Lead mining has gone on in Derbyshire since Roman times, and from the Middle Ages onwards was vital to the economic and social development of the Peak District. Disturbed ground is evident across the orefield of the limestone plateau and in all there are around 25,000 lead mining shafts. Mineral extraction has had a great impact on the outward appearance of the White Peak, from the remnant hillocks of old lead workings to giant craters and scars in the ground made by quarrying in more recent years. Evidence of centuries of mineral extraction exists in the countryside surrounding the River Bradford. What is not evident is the drainage undertaken to reach lead ore from below the water table from the late seventeenth to the early nineteenth century. This has had a critical impact on the rivers of the White Peak including the River Bradford.

As early as 1642, 20,000 named people were associated with lead mining in Derbyshire. In the Derbyshire Dales the existence of lead mining as the major employer of men throughout the eighteenth century and early nineteenth century consolidated the rural communities of the area, despite the loss of the commons. The stability of the population of villages such as Youlgrave, Middleton and Alport owes much to the gruelling work and immense wealth generated by what lay under the ground rather than the living to be made above ground on the farms of the White Peak. The fortunes of the villages along the River Bradford are inextricably linked to the industry. Lead mining gave Youlgrave one version of its name – *Auldgroove* (*groove* is an old name for a mine), its fine church and even the former name of one of its pubs 'The Pig of Lead' (now The George).

Lead is so important to the story of the River Bradford and its communities that Part 3 of the book explores this ancient industry in more detail.

Bradford Dale and Youlgrave viewed from the east

Part 2

The River Bradford: a Journey along the River and through the Past

'*The river is within us*'

T. S. Eliot, *Dry Salvages, The Four Quartets*, 1941

Dawn on the River Bradford at Brookleton

The journey along the River Bradford follows the stream from where it first comes to light as a series of springs, to its end, where it joins the River Lathkill. The entire length of the Bradford watercourse is a mere four miles from the source in Gratton Dale to the confluence with the River Lathkill at Alport.

Over time, parts of the river have had a variety of names including Rollow Brook or Roller Brook, Bradford Rivulet and, latterly, River Bradford. The names give us a clue to what the Bradford once was – a brook, a stream or a rivulet, rising from springs in a remote valley to run through deep gorges, quiet dells and open meadows. The Bradford's status as a river is, perhaps, owed to the past uses people have made of this limestone stream over many hundreds of years.

Where the River Rises

Gratton Dale, where the River Bradford rises, lies due south of Youlgrave. It is a dry valley typical of the Dales. Gratton Dale, together with Long Dale at its southern end, forms a deep, V-shaped depression in the high ground of Gratton Moor, Smerrill Moor and Elton Common.

These dales, with their steep sides and wild rough pastures full of wildflowers, are havens for wildlife. While dry for much of the year, there is a concrete tank from which water flows all year round, sustained by a spring from the limestone where it overlies a lava bed. During wet periods, the shivering, dimpling surface of a shallow muddy puddle in the shadowed depths of the dale make the first daylight show of the waters of the River Bradford. The path that runs along the rocky floor of the dale then forms a streambed. In winter and after heavy rain, the stream is also fed by springs from the dale sides.

The water flows under the lane at the end of the dale and emerges at Dale End where it flows into marshy ground lying north of the lane linking Elton with Middleton-by-Youlgrave. This area sometimes bubbles with the activity of mating frogs and can be golden with marsh marigolds in spring or with mimulus in summer. Here the stream forms a valuable wetland habitat in a farming landscape in which so much land is drained.

The stream flows west alongside the lane at Dale End opposite the Old Cheese Factory, a large house that still goes by that name. In the days before centralised milk collection and distribution, local cheese production made good use of milk from neighbouring farms in the more remote country areas. Retired local farmer Henry Brocklehurst visited the Gratton cheese factory as a child:

'I can just remember going to the cheese factory with my grandfather. We would go in the pony and trap. I saw the vat with all the milk in, he must have lifted me up to look in it.'

According to Henry an accidental spill of whey into the stream from the 'factory' in the 1920s had disastrous results, contaminating the River Bradford for a time.

The gathering pens of an old sheepwash opposite the cheese factory would indicate that the flow of the stream here was once sufficient for this purpose. A much larger sheepwash is located downstream at Middleton.

Left : The packhorse bridge over the River Bradford
Above : Gratton Dale where the river rises
Right : The stream in full flow from Gratton Dale

An ancient trackway used in the Middle Ages once passed close by the southern end of the Bradford. The 'Old Way' ran from Derby to Manchester and linked the upland villages of the Peak District. It followed the course of the lane from Elton to Dale End, forded the stream and then went through marshy ground above Gratton Grange Farm. The route then descended through the fields to meet what is now the track from Lowfields Farm which re-crosses the stream and climbs the hill to Middleton where *'the old hollow-way is very plain'*. [7]

The water meadows of Gratton Grange Farm surround the stream as it flows on north-west towards a hidden dale that is one of the most mysterious of all in Derbyshire.

Marshy ground at Gratton Grange Farm

View north-east across the River Bradford's hidden dale

The Hidden Dale

The first dale that the stream runs through is called variously Roller, Rollow or Fishpond Dale. Some maps refer to it as Smerrill or Fishpond Wood. There is no right of way now through this crescent-shaped and deeply wooded dale but this was once a busy and thriving place. There are caves and rock shelters here that could indicate human usage many thousands of years ago. However, it is the remnants of medieval habitation and use that are of particular interest. The current Ordnance Survey map refers to Fishpond Wood and to this upper part of the river as Rowlow Brook. The Arkwright Society calls this dale Fishpond Dale and there are several records that allude to the pools, which are still evident, as medieval fishponds that were maintained and managed by the inhabitants of Smerrill Grange, situated high above the southern edge of the dale. During the Middle Ages, in areas far from the sea, fish from rivers and streams provided a vital source of food all year round, as did the cress beds that were cultivated by the monastic granges. This may help explain the presence of so many monastic settlements located close by the streams and rivers of Youlgrave and Middleton.

Smerrill Grange Farm was close to the vanished medieval village of Smerrill, which was also located above the dale. There is scant evidence of this now, other than some raised earth and a scattering of stones.

[7] Dodd and Dodd, *Peakland Roads and Trackways*, p59.
[8] Information from Rhodri Thomas PDNPA.

But plants can help tell the story of the past. The green hellebore (*Helleborus viridis*) is a rare native perennial found in only a few sites in the White Peak and, according to the New Atlas of British Flora *'has been grown in gardens since medieval times'*. It grows high up on the dale side close by the medieval settlement and has also been found close to Conksbury Bridge. It was grown for medicinal purposes and is a living link to people who once lived here. Another nationally scarce plant, the Yellow Star-of-Bethlehem, grows along the dale bottom.[8]

Rowlow Brook emerges from the mouth of the dale below what is now Smerrill Grange Farm. The valley widens out at this point and the stream flows due north, bordered on the west by a field that rises steeply towards Weaddow Lane (the lane between Gratton and Middleton which meets the Old Way). The name Weaddow refers to castrated male sheep, 'wethers', that were presumably driven along here in large numbers in the past. On the east bank, sheer limestone cliffs rise from the water and are mirrored in the stream, creating a typical dales landscape in miniature. At this point it is possible to view the mysterious 'Rollow Dale' from a public footpath that runs above Rusden Wood.

Left : Smerrill Grange Farm
Below : Rowlow Brook in winter

Rusden Wood – the 'Rogues Den'

Rusden Wood, located less than a mile south of Middleton, is in the care of the Peak District National Park Authority. This is a place of great interest. A footpath runs through the bottom of the wood, in wet periods becoming a stream that feeds into the Bradford. This little wooded dale, a deep cleft in the limestone, was named, intriguingly, 'Rogues Den' in a Manor Survey map of 1799 and the stream was called Smerrill Brook. Within its short length are five rock shelters, two caves, one collapsed cave and a fissure.[9] The likelihood of human habitation or hideaways in this dale is self-evident. The modern name Rusden Wood had formerly been attached to another piece of woodland close by. The continuation of this dale ascends west across Weaddow Lane and up into what is now Kenslow Wood. This was also formerly known as Rogues Den. One can only surmise the origins of this name, but it is possible that instead of this being a place where dubious, criminal types lurked, it may have been a sanctuary or hide-out for religious nonconformists, or for unemployed, impoverished people persecuted by laws imposed under Elizabeth I that designated such people as 'Rogues and Vagabonds.'[10]

The dale floor is carpeted with celandine and wood anemone in spring. Woodruff and wood sorrel also grow here. Where Rusden Wood adjoins the Rollow Brook, the narrow waterway flows through a boggy dell where water avens grows. Dippers can be seen here occasionally and water voles have frequented this secluded stretch in the recent past.

Left : Detail of Manor Survey map of Middleton 1799 (reproduced with permission of Haddon Estate)
Right : Rusden Wood

[9] *A Conservation Audit of Archaeological Cave Resources in the Peak District and Yorkshire Dales*, University of Sheffield (ARCUS). [10] In the *Statute for the punishment of Vagabonds* (1572) it was decreed that '*if such person or persons be duly convicted of his or her roguish or vagabond trade of life, either by inquest of office, or by the testimony of two honest and credible witnesses upon their oaths, that then immediately he or she shall be adjudged to be grievously whipped and burnt through the gristle of the right ear with a hot iron, manifesting his or her roguish kind of life, and his or her punishment received for the same, which judgment shall also presently be executed, except some honest person will of his charity be contented presently to take such offender into his service for one whole year next following*'.

Roller Brook

The stream is little more than a ditch as it flows north through the wide and shallow valley that lies between Hopping Farm and the gently rising land south of Middleton. In the Manor Survey plan of 1799 this meandering stream is called Roller Brook. It is unfenced and there are several fords across parts of the stream where cattle cross. In wetter springs and in summer the marshy margins of the stream are host to the increasingly rare ragged robin. This wet pasture was once good territory for nesting lapwing and other waders such as snipe. Visiting mandarin ducks come to this section of the river most years, but rarely stay to nest. Because this stretch of the stream lies away from the footpath and the frequent intrusion of dogs it has, in the past, been an important area for a population of water voles. Drought and flood and the heavy tread of cattle crossing the stream or drinking there have now damaged the banks which were home to water voles, and made this an unreliable habitat for them, despite the area's relative seclusion.

The stream runs through this valley in a line which can be seen just above the barn in the foreground

Henry Brocklehurst remembers the rich wildlife in this patch in former times:

'There used to be a lot of curlews. The last ones that I saw nesting were at the bottom of Goldyslack on the right up Weaddow Lane. There were a lot of skylarks, curlews and peewits. When we were ploughing at Lowfields with a horse-drawn plough, there was any amount of peewits, and we were forever stopping and dodging their nests.'

The stream widens below Hopping Farm and is prone to flooding. When waterlogged, the stream can flow right over the medieval clapper bridge that has stood here for centuries as a crossing place from north to south. In spring and summer the shallow rock ledges that border the stream on the south bank are festooned with wild flowers that thrive on the thin soils of the limestone bedrock. Meadow saxifrage, lady's smock, salad burnet, birdsfoot trefoil, lady's mantle, stonecrop, rock-roses and wild thyme have all grown here.

Flooded brook below Hopping Farm

Clapper bridge at the southern end of the dale

Water meadows below Hopping Farm

To the north of the clapper bridge a steep bank rises above the path that leads to the dale. The varied habitat around the confluence of streams and footpaths includes at this point wildflower meadow, boggy ground, stream, woodland and scrub.

The bank above the footpath into the dale has been unaltered by farming practice over decades. Untreated and unmown, it is host to a great profusion of wildflowers that were once common in the Derbyshire Dales: knapweed, betony, devilsbit scabious, field scabious, centaury, St John's wort and agrimony. From summer through to autumn this bank hums with insects and is the best place to see butterflies for miles around.

This bank extends into a narrow strip of woodland consisting mainly of scots pine, sycamore and larch. Beyond it there is rough, untreated pasture dotted with scrubby hawthorn bushes and brambles.

This whole area combines a great variety of habitats and is rich in biodiversity. Summer visitors such as whitethroat, chiffchaff, garden warbler, blackcap, redstart and spotted flycatchers can all be seen here. Buzzards nest nearby and kestrels hunt here, indicating a good population of small mammals.

The stream, running far below the footpath, remains undisturbed and after a long period of absence from the River Bradford, water voles returned to this stretch of the stream in 2008, enjoying the dense cover of reeds and banks that are out of the range of roaming cattle.

Spotted flycatcher

Ragged robin

Green-veined white on devilsbit scabious

Peacock on field scabious

Water Vole *(Arvicola amphibius)*

The water vole is Britain's fastest-declining wild mammal and is now extinct in many parts of the country. It has suffered from loss of habitat and from predation by introduced American mink.

Water voles are rodents that are often called water rats. They are only distantly related to brown rats and, while a similar size, are different in appearance with a bluntly rounded nose that is typical of the vole family. They live their lives on the banks of rivers, streams or ponds and feed almost entirely on waterside plants. Patches of 'grazed' sedges, grasses or reeds near the water can indicate their presence, but it is the distinct 'plop' of a water vole's sudden dive into the water that can reveal where it is. Its fur is a rich brown colour and its chubby body can appear to be oddly flattened out as it swims along a stream.

The water vole's home range is very limited. The male occupies around 130 metres of riverbank and is often sedentary. But the female, while occupying a smaller home range, may move on to establish new territory elsewhere. They mark the limits of their home range with small heaps of droppings (latrines).

Water voles build their nests with grasses below ground in burrows alongside the stream, or at the base of waterside plants. The burrows have openings above and below the waterline. Four or five litters of about five young can be raised between March and October.

The sound of a water vole's plop into the river, or the sight of one swimming, grooming itself, or just sitting on a mud bank, were familiar to anyone walking alongside the River Bradford until about fifteen years ago. After disappearing altogether for several years, water voles returned to Bradford Dale around ten years ago. But while there are still signs and occasional sightings, seeing a water vole now is a rare treat. They are shy creatures that cannot tolerate much disturbance and the constant pressure of high visitor numbers has not helped them to re-establish themselves.

They are now fully protected by law under *The Wildlife and Countryside Act 1981, section 9*, with special provisions for this species added in 2008. The Act makes '*damage or destruction, or disturbance while … occupying places of shelter*' a criminal offence.

The water vole's habitat along the River Bradford has been disrupted by roaming cattle and by extreme weather. Floods have washed away their nests and burrow systems in the bank sides. Drought has removed both their food source and their habitat as semi-aquatic mammals. Now that the river's flow is restored there are peaceful sections of the river that are ideal for water voles and signs that they may still thrive there.[11]

[11] The Wildlife Trusts are working on protecting and increasing habitats for water voles and dealing with predators in various locations. They are also being re-introduced into certain areas, with some success. The river keeper Warren Slaney undertakes the work of habitat renewal and predator control on the River Bradford.

Fulwood's Rock

Descending the metal steps into the beginning of the dale, another world opens up and once again we are in territory of age-old usage of the river and matters of high historical drama.

Immediately to the right of the steps into the dale, a rock has collapsed from the limestone cliff above leaving a gap behind it. This deep cleft in the rock was used as a hiding place during the Civil War, but it became a deadly trap for Royalist Sir Christopher Fulwood in 1643.

Sir Christopher was the eldest son of Sir George Fulwood who was Lord of the Manor in Middleton, his family having made their fortune from lead mining. His home, Middleton Castle, was a sizeable mansion, which was situated above and overlooking the dale. Little remains of this today other than some ivy-clad walls and a causeway that formed the drive to the house.

Like his barrister father Sir George, Christopher practised law in London, living in Middleton-by-Youlgrave when not professionally engaged in the city. He was chairman of the local magistrates in Bakewell and in this role was considered to be a fair and impartial man of law and generally well regarded in the area.

While much of Derbyshire supported the Parliamentary cause, Fulwood was a Royalist and had sufficient influence to muster a force of 1,100 lead miners on Tideswell Moor in 1642 as a lifeguard for the King. This posed a very serious threat to the Parliamentarians and spurred their local leader Sir John Gell into action. Gell, who was the Puritan squire of Hopton Hall, sent men to capture Fulwood in the autumn of 1643. Being warned of an imminent attack, Fulwood managed to escape from the castle into Bradford Dale and to hide in the rock crevice in the 'gooseholme' where he was shot and fatally injured by his pursuers. He was taken as a prisoner to the Roundhead garrison town of Lichfield but he died en route at Calton in Staffordshire on 16 November 1643.

Fulwood's Rock in the Middleton gooseholme

Middleton Gooseholme

Like so many of the limestone dales, Middleton Dale is dominated by ash and sycamore. However the high cliffs that rise to the fields of Hopping Farm are covered in beech and wych-elm, which cling to the almost vertical dale sides and provide this part of the dale with a rich area of autumn colour.

At the opening or 'mouth' of the dale, the enclosure made by cliffs and trees has formed a kind of bowl that floods in wet periods. This area was once referred to as the gooseholme. A 'holme' is an area of rich flat pasture beside a river and this gooseholme was part of the common land on which the locals were able to graze their stock of geese from medieval times. The area is now in the process of re-naturalising, becoming a reed bed, colonised by a few self-sown willows and the dominant plant, reed canarygrass. In summer, nettles and great willowherb grow among the canarygrass to tower above the footpath through the gooseholme. Although flooded in wet seasons, this area has returned almost to a marsh with the stream weaving a narrow course through it.

There used to be commons all along the dale. All of the commons of Bradford Dale were lost to the people with the Youlgrave and Middleton Enclosure Award of 1818 that followed on the Act of 1815. They were allocated to the Duke of Rutland. In the Manor Survey Map of 1799 *(see map on inside front cover)* Mootlow Common is evident on the south-facing bank of the dale and Coldwell End Common is marked along the steep north-facing bank.

In the early nineteenth century the old gooseholme was cleared out and a dam built to provide a water supply for a new mill.

Left : Beech trees cling to the steep dale side
Right : Middleton gooseholme

Footbridge across the outflow from Middleton Spring

Middleton Spring or Well Head

The path through the gooseholme crosses the stream over a footbridge then leads across the outflow of the spring that rises here. The hollow formed by the natural stone archway contains a perforated metal ball attached to an iron pipe that the spring flowed into. This metal ball is very visible when the water level is low, which has been the case for much of the time over recent years, both summer and winter. In former times the water that was drawn from this spring would have supplied much of Middleton.

For many locals and visitors familiar with the area, the flow of water from this tiny cave indicates the health of the local water supply. When dried out, which it so often is in the summer, the small strip of stony ground that emerges from the cliff below Middleton makes us wonder when the rain will come to replenish the spring. This dark corner of the dale is a clue to what lies beneath us – the complex system of fractures and water-widened fissures that filter what falls from the sky. With the soaking of ground, the seeping, draining, dripping and eventual flooding of subterranean spaces, the levels rise, the water table is restored and flow from the spring rises to the light once more. Here symbolism and material fact demonstrate and support our ancient understanding of springs as the source of life.

A track leads west up to Middleton through a deeply wooded gorge. This ancient trackway is overhung by a limestone bluff with further cliffs that can be glimpsed through the trees on the north side. On the south side old quarry workings are evident. In spring the floor of this offshoot of the dale is carpeted with lesser celandine.

An illustration of Middleton Mill, courtesy of Robinson plc who bought a pill box business that operated from Fletchers Mill in 1839, from *The Firm of Robinson and Sons, Ltd.*

Industry in Middleton Dale

The waterways that flowed from the hills of the Pennines set in motion the wheels of the early Industrial Revolution. It was water power that drove the machines that made steel, fabrics, tools and foods and developed the towns and cities of Sheffield, Manchester, Leeds, Bradford and Derby, in turn making Britain the 'workshop of the world'. These great urban centres of northern and central England with their diverse industries are a far cry from the tranquil Middleton Dale, but in the earliest days of water-powered mechanisation this place was a hive of industry and innovation.

It requires some imaginative effort to envisage what Middleton Dale must have been like in the mid nineteenth century. Lead mining was the principal industry in this area from the middle of the seventeenth century and remained the main employer of men for over two hundred years. It also employed both women and children.

During the eighteenth and nineteenth centuries the major occupation of women and children in Middleton and surrounding villages was lacemaking. Women worked in their own homes as 'outworkers' producing both very fine work in silk and cruder work in cotton. It is possible that there was a connection between the lacemakers of Middleton and the establishment of bobbin manufacture in the dale. Lace bobbins were of the finest size and these were among the range produced in Middleton.

At the opening of the gorge that leads up to the village of Middleton, on the right-hand side, stands the ruin of an old building with stone mullions that are still visible and are all that remains of what was once a large and imposing mill.

In 1822 a dam was built on the site of the old gooseholme to drive a nine-ton water wheel that was to power a new mill in Middleton Dale. It is clear from the contemporary illustration shown here that this was a large mill with three long rows of windows. This scale of operation pales when compared with Arkwright's mills at Cromford and Matlock Bath, especially the huge Masson Mill that was powered by the mighty flow of the Derwent. But the same entrepreneurial spirit was clearly present in harnessing the power of the little Bradford brook at the height of the Industrial Revolution.

This mill initially made red tape for Government and legal use. While red tape is still in use today, we are more used to referring to the symbolic meaning of the red tape than the real material used to tie up documents. The Victorians were heavily engaged in administrative bureaucracy, as many spheres of human activity were developing at an unprecedented rate and required regulation and legislation. So here in little Middleton Dale great and minor affairs of law and state were being served.

Women and children were employed in this factory, as they were employed in factories all over Britain, very often in terrible conditions. In *Some Account of Youlgrave, Middleton and Alport* - a booklet produced by members of the Youlgrave Women's Institute in 1931 – there is a sobering reflection on the hardships of child mill workers in the early nineteenth century:

'*Romantic the scenery may be but there would be nothing romantic about life for the children who worked there for so long before. The early days of that century were the very worst as far as conditions of work were concerned … an old writer in 1801 … describes, with satisfaction, watching the children coming away at seven in the evening, in Cromford. They had been at work for more than twelve hours except for their dinner hour, which was forty minutes, beginning at noon. For these long hours a boy of ten or eleven years old was paid 3/6 at the end of the week and the little girls' wages were 2/3. Beautiful surroundings, although a help, did not counteract the evil effects of such terrible and deadening toil in the midst of machinery.*'

Children who worked in the textile mills of Manchester and elsewhere toiled for up to seventeen hours a day and the Derbyshire Dales have their own shameful history of child exploitation and abuse akin to slavery, as we can see in accounts of child workers' conditions at Litton Mill.[12]

The business was sold in 1839 to the chemist John Bradbury Robinson to manufacture cardboard pill boxes. This business later moved to Chesterfield to become the famous Robinson's packaging business, which went on to make wound dressings for use in the Crimean War. The company is now a global enterprise whose embryonic beginnings were in Middleton Dale.

The mill later produced bobbins of various sizes for both the cotton industry (for use in Arkwright's mills) and for lacemaking. But this business had a very short life and by the 1850s production of tapes, boxes and bobbins was history. In Francis White's *History and Gazetteer of Derbyshire* of 1857 there is a reference to the mill, but it was no longer making bobbins:

'In the romantic glen of the Lathkill [sic], is a factory formerly employed in making tapes, but now used partly as a day school and partly as a colour manufactory.'

[12] The conditions of child workers at Litton Mill in Cressbrook were atrocious. Young orphans were taken there from London and worked so hard and for such long hours that many died, including some who took their own lives rather than endure the toil and beatings any longer. It was an account from a child mill-worker, Robert Blincoe, who had worked at Litton Mill, that caused a national outcry when it was first published in 1828 and eventually led to a government investigation into factory conditions and later reforms. It is unlikely that local children with families in Middleton and Youlgrave suffered as those defenceless children of the Litton Mill did but it is unrealistic to imagine that any factory workers' conditions at this time would be considered tolerable today.

Middleton Dale mid-winter

Middleton sheepwash

Pumping Water to Middleton

The water power formerly used to work the tape and bobbin mill was later used to pump water up to Middleton. The great waterwheel was twelve feet in diameter by eight feet wide and was housed inside the mill building. As the water supply became insufficient to power the pump, first a petrol engine was used and later an electric motor. The man who was in charge of the pump for a good many years was Don Bateman. Don was born on 30 April 1924, lived in Youlgrave for most of his life, and worked as village blacksmith in Middleton during and after the Second World War. Later he also worked for the Waterhouses at Middleton Hall and was responsible for keeping a water supply going up to Middleton by checking the pump every day. He explains:

'I'm the past master of the Middleton pump. I used to be on the water wheel and the pump. The spring at Middleton … under the rock, it flowed from there into the dam and that drove the water wheel. In the (engine) shed was a piston pump and it went at 36 strokes a minute. It must not go any faster. That pumped water right up above Middleton Hall and this Middleton Hall reservoir fed Middleton Hall and Lomberdale Hall, about twenty-seven houses and seven farms.

I started blacksmithing during the war. I was exempt from military service because someone had to shoe the horses and repair machines for farmers, because they had to keep going for food. I started working on the pump after the war. I used to go down every day. Then I put a block of grease on the joints and then I went down every other day. It didn't have to go fast or it would have wrecked the pump you see. The shafts were massive, eight inches in diameter. It was all cast iron. Twiggs had it as scrap. The wheel was in the old cotton mill. There's just bits of ruin now.'

This system of pumping water up to Middleton was in place for a long time, but the spring water supply began to fail in the 1930s and another source was found. The engine house or shed that Don mentions was in place at the end of the nineteenth century when it was marked as such on an Ordnance Survey Map of 1900.

Sheepwash

At the bottom end of what was once the gooseholme are walled enclosures, which are the well-preserved remains of a sheepwash. During times when wool was highly valued, many villages had sheepwashes so that sheep could be gathered and their fleeces roughly washed before shearing. The system of gathering pens has remained intact and was still in use until the 1950s.

Henry Brocklehurst was born at Green Farm and moved with his family to Castle Farm when he was two years old. He lived at Castle Farm as a child and then farmed there for fifty years:

'My great-great-great-grandfather farmed in Middleton and my mother's side of the family have also lived in Middleton ever since. Nearly all my working life was spent at Castle Farm. That goes back to the days of carting water up out of the dale. At Castle farm we were one of the last two farms to dip sheep in the dale right up to the last time in the 1950s. You had to go to the estate office and get the key that you turned to get the water into the sheepwash. When you finished, you shut it off and it came down the side or through the race where the old mills were. The sheep came from a long way off. They drove them down from Friden. In those days you got so much more for your wool if it was washed. And then things changed and you got the same price so that's why farmers stopped washing because there was no benefit really.'

Boathouse Dam

The top dam in the dale was once called the Boathouse Dam, as the Waterhouse family from Middleton Hall kept a boat here. This deeply enclosed part of the dale runs from south-east to north-west below steep and densely wooded banks. The weedy and often brilliant emerald green of the marshy dam surrounds the meandering thread of the stream.

Henry Brocklehurst remembers his childhood in Middleton:

'We had a really good time as children. You made your own pleasure. We were sledging, playing marbles, or tracking round the woods and the dale. You put arrows where you'd gone, leaving clues. We could roam anywhere. We had a fair few huts we built in the woods and the dale. They were built of stones with a roof. The children had more or less got it to themselves. We used to roam for hours.

I think people in the village thought of the dale as their treasured spot and there's a lot of people have had their ashes scattered there.

Middleton Corn Mill

Below the next dam a broad bridge crosses the river and leads to a steep path out of the dale. On the north side of the river a level area that is overgrown with trees and scrub is the site of Middleton Corn Mill. The mill leat can still be seen running alongside this dam. In 1876 the mill was managed by Joseph and Alfred Johnson. The Johnsons also ran the Alport Flour Mill *(see page 71)*. The Middleton mill replaced a much earlier mill, the dam of which is clearly visible on a map of 1799 at what appears to be the site of the old gooseholme. A corn mill is also mentioned in the Domesday Survey.

The Victorian mill was demolished and the stone used to build cottages in Middleton in 1914.

There are two solitary and rather stunted oak trees below the Corn Mill bridge. Their presence here indicates a deposit of less alkaline soil (oaks struggle to grow on limestone). These old trees support lichens found almost nowhere else in the Peak District.[13]

The most substantial built relic of the past along the dale is a wheelwright's shop that once stood just north of the old Corn Mill. Local people say that red-hot wheels made in the workshop were rolled down into the river to temper them and make them 'true'. The ruined wheelwright's shop is all that is left of the busy world that Middleton Dale once was.

An ancient path known to locals as Corn Mill Lane, now part of the Limestone Way, passes the ruin and rises in a steep zigzag. The high retaining wall that supports this path shows how important this track was. It is a place that evokes the busy past. The stones are slippery, polished over years by the tread of mill workers, lead miners, and agricultural labourers. The path leads to Roughwood Hollow, which is rumoured to be haunted. A man's skeleton was uncovered here in a rock crevice by men who were excavating the road. His remains were found together with his lead mining tools.[14]

In the little valley below the retaining wall of the path, the nationally scarce narrow-leaved bittercress grows in its ideal conditions of damp calcareous woodland.

Below the ruined wheelwright's shop, a narrow pathway known locally as Spring Lane strikes off to the right. This follows the river along the north side, passing several springs and watercress beds that are often picked by locals as food for free from the river. This marshy area is dominated by lesser pond sedge and supports a wide range of invertebrates. The springs rise here because a layer of toadstone outcrops on the valley floor, forming an impermeable layer so that water flows out horizontally above it.

Top left : Middleton Corn Mill bridge

Left : Middleton Corn Mill circa 1890 (photo courtesy of *Our Middleton*)

---

[13] Information on lichens from Rhodri Thomas PDNPA.
[14] Middleton Village History Group, *Our Middleton*, p66.

Top left : Corn Mill Dam   **Top middle** : One of the two oak trees in the dale
Bottom left : Corn Mill Lane   **Bottom middle** : Ruins of the old wheelwright's shop
Right : Watercress beds

Little grebe or dabchick

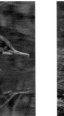

Female goosander

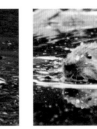

Shoveler

Water vole

As the direction of the dale alters, a path rises away from the river and climbs up through dense ash and sycamore woods to reach the western end of Youlgrave – Coldwell End. Dog mercury covers much of the steep ground surrounding the path. This part of the dale was formerly Coldwell Common. The ruins of a limekiln and other buildings are concealed in what is now dense scrub through which there is no right of way. The relative seclusion offered by this south-facing bank makes this a haven for wildlife, and timid dabchicks (little grebe) and other waterfowl frequent this side of the river. Occasional visitors to the dale, including goosander, shoveler and once, notably, a water rail all preferred to stay close to the north side of the river. On rare occasions, tufted ducks have succeeded in breeding here, but kept close to the bank. When owners allow their dogs into the river, these birds give up, move on and are lost to Bradford Dale.

From both Spring Lane and Roughwood Hollow you can see through the trees the towering reef-knoll limestone outcrops of Moatlow Knob, the gleaming dams and sometimes rushing weirs.

Along the main path on the south bank, a gate links to a boundary wall that encloses the densely wooded, precipitous bank above the top dam. Beyond this, the hillside rises steeply through territory that is typical of the limestone dales. Scree slopes flank from Moatlow Knob. Mature ash and sycamore trees and saplings cling to the steep and stony banks. Exposed low cliffs and shallow rock ledges can be seen all along the north-facing dale side and reveal the underlying direction and structure of the limestone bedrock. The bluff that descends below Moatlow Knob forms a sudden turn in the direction of Bradford Dale and the flow of the river now runs almost from west to east. The gorge of Bradford Dale was cut as water eroded through shales then limestone, exposing the weather-resistant reef knoll of Moatlow. The trapped water then flowed sideways resulting in this sharp bend in the dale. A third dam crosses the river at this point.

Moatlow Knob

Third dam

Moatlow

The hill-top area called Moatlow lies within Hopping Farm and this area is full of old lead mining shafts and workings. In summer the old lead rakes with their mounds and hollows are carpeted with a rich variety of wild flowers and grasses that are tolerant to metal *(see page 68)*. Below the south-facing hill, the terraced strip lynchets that can be seen from afar offer rare evidence of medieval strip farming, a remnant of past lives.

An old path runs up the north-facing dale side and extends to the high edge of the dale, close to Moatlow Knob. Locals sometimes call it the 'Saxon Path'. Others have called it 'Lovers' Lane'. While its exact origins are unknown, its route leading to Moatlow may be significant. Research indicates that 'Moatlow' may have been a meeting place from Anglo-Saxon times: *'Some of the principal courts or moot sites of the Wapentakes are revealed by place names …*[such as] *Moatlow – Youlgreave'.*[15]

In this part of the dale a few cattle are turned out through autumn and winter to browse on the dense scrub and to graze the steep dale sides. The exposed grassy banks on the north side of the dale are host to many limestone-loving plants, notably cowslips, and some orchids grow along the higher pastures. Lower down are other unusual species such as Town-Hall clock (moschatel) and twayblade (an orchid). Mosses grow here that are considered scarce in the Peak District. Wild valerian can still be seen growing along the river and on the bank sides. It is said that this herb was once gathered by herbalists from Sheffield and Chesterfield as a remedy for stress and insomnia. Further along the dale above the fourth dam, on a flat area on the open north-facing dale side, there was an old lead mine.

Top left : Moatlow viewed from the south
Bottom left : Wild flowers on the old Moatlow lead workings

[15] *Derbyshire Archeological Journal*, Vol 102, 1982. Wapentake derives from the Old Norse '*wapnatak*' meaning the 'taking of weapons'. A Wapentake was an administrative division of the counties under Danelaw corresponding to the 'hundreds' elsewhere. At an assembly or 'moot', votes could be cast by a show of weapons.

The last of the six dams in the dale can be approached here from the village side via a steep path through the trees. This was the route that some village children used to take to their beloved dale. Chris Wragg has lived in Youlgrave all his life and, like most villagers, the place holds many memories for him:

'The dale was a very safe place. You used to go either as a gang or, many a time, I'd go on my own. You never saw anybody when I was a kid, just the odd angler or two, the gamekeeper, river keeper and water bailiff. He used to come along on his bike and you had to get your fishing line (which we had wound round a Brillo tin) and put your things away, and just walk away and whistle. He knew what you were up to. We would try catching fish with a rabbit hang (a snare), but it was very hard gauging the right width and depth.'

Above : Moss-covered scree below Moatlow
Right : The bottom dams of the Bradford

'As long as you were on your own you'd hear a plop and you knew it was a water vole dropping into the water. And it would surface ten or fifteen feet further across on the other bank.

We used to build camps in the dale. We'd go out first thing in the morning and spend all day in there because you could in those days. We made bows and arrows and spears because the materials were there. I used to paddle a lot because there were bullyheads and spinks – a very small fish smaller than minnow and they did take some catching. We used to build a bit of a pool, drop them in and then at the end of the day we'd see how many we'd caught then open it up and let them go. At one time you could get frogspawn anywhere on the dale.

In the tunnels below the shuttles at the weir there's a board. When it was fairly dry and the board was up you could wade up in your wellies and you could always find a dipper's nest under the tunnel, every time. I don't think we disturbed them and we never took any eggs from the nest.

I spent a big part of my childhood there. You always had a different way to get to places. You just went anywhere, where the sheep had made a path for you. We used to explore almost everywhere, but we never went up Nelly Long Arm, people always said there was a mineshaft part way down so we never actually dared go in. We used to try and run up the scree slope to Moatlow Knob, but you couldn't do it.

It was so peaceful and you could just stand or sit there and listen and hear the songbirds. No matter where you looked at one time you'd always find either a song thrush or a blackbird's nest.'

'Nelly Long Arm' that Chris refers to is an entry into the hillside on the southern side of the dale that leads into a tunnel. The name was probably devised as an early health and safety measure, with local parents warning their children that should they venture into the tunnel, the witch Nelly would reach out to drag them in. The tunnel is a horizontal entry into an old mine which is now home to cave-dwelling species of tissue moth

and herald moth and to the cave spider *Meta menardi*.[16] Beneath the river at this point lies a deep drainage sough, the poetically named Pyenets Nest Level, that is causing the river to leak.[17]

Below the weir from the bottom dam the river runs almost naturally, despite the canalised sides that straighten the course of what would once have been a meandering stream. In this section of the dale, the trees on the north side overhang the water and sometimes kingfishers survey the river from these branches. The shallow waters run over and around big stones, making islands that dippers can rest on and where they can preen or sing. Grey wagtails also visit this stretch, as it is rich with invertebrates lurking on or below the surface of the water. Both dippers and wagtails can be seen here searching for food by turning over the leaves that fall into the river in autumn.

Far left : The Bradford below Coldwell End in spring **Above** : Grey wagtail

---

[16] Information from Rhodri Thomas PDNPA.
[17] 'Pyenet' is an old Derbyshire name for the magpie, for which there are numerous regional variations.

Dipper (*Cinclus cinclus*)

The dipper is the iconic bird of the streams and rivers of the Peak District. This enchanting bird is evident all year round and we are especially privileged to see it on the River Bradford, as it is more often associated with fast flowing, shallow waters of upland streams and rivers.

Dippers are unique in the bird world for their behaviours and habits. They are dapper little birds, marginally smaller and dumpier than a blackbird, with a dusky dark brown plumage that appears to be black from a distance. By contrast they have a startling white bib that extends from the throat down to the belly. They can be seen all along the River Bradford and, when perched on a favourite rock, execute a kind of regular bobbing and curtseying from which they get their name. Dippers have a characteristic stance, with their short tail held erect, rather like a wren. They have short wings and powerful legs. When flying fast and low, skimming the river, their sharp, loud call can often be heard in the dale, cutting through the sounds of rushing water.

Dippers feed well from the river all year round on invertebrates, worms, freshwater shrimps and small fish. The Bradford is rich in invertebrates, and the caddis fly, especially, is a major food source for both dipper and grey wagtail. A dipper constantly forages, turning over leaves or searching the riverbed by walking along the bottom of the stream with its powerful claws gripping the streambed. When they catch small fish such as bullheads, they will pause on a rock to beat the fish's head to kill it and then peck at it; unlike the kingfisher, which will turn a fish so that it goes down head first in one beakful.

It is fascinating to watch a dipper quietly working the river as it disappears under water then suddenly bobs up to perch on a stone. Dippers can swim and use their short wings as flippers. They are able to stay underwater for up to half a minute. Sometimes, when scouring the riverbed in shallow water, a dipper may be encapsulated in a bubble of water before emerging to shake off the droplets.

All year round, but especially so in the autumn and winter months, a low, warbling and melodious song can be heard emanating from the river. Both male and female dippers will perch, sometimes for extended periods, often in a shady spot, and sing continuously, the song merging with the gurgling and rushing sounds of the stream. The dipper is seeking to establish or maintain territory or to attract a mate. It has a constant food source year round so there is no energy gap through the winter and dippers can begin courtship and nest building very early on. Courtship behaviour can begin as early as October. The nest is made from grasses and mosses and is often built using the cover provided by man-made structures, such as bridges or weirs. A pair of dippers usually raises two broods and the first clutch of eggs are laid in early March.

At one time, each section of Bradford Dale had its nesting pair of dippers and they could be seen all year round. It is surprising that they seem to cope with the heavy riverside traffic of people and dogs, but they will not tolerate intrusion into their territory, the river itself. Now after a period of absence some have returned to the River Bradford, but in lesser numbers.

The old fisherman's cottage circa 1900 (photo supplied by Gordon Coupe)

Bats hunt along the dale and can be seen at dusk skimming the water for insects or flitting around high in the ash tree canopy. There are probably several species of bats, but certainly Pipistrelle (which occasionally fly in full daylight) and Daubentons are present in Bradford Dale – a place that literally hums with insect activity in summer.

Quite often in autumn or winter a loud shriek will startle an evening walker and the air will seem filled with grey ghostly wings as a heron, disturbed while fishing the shallows, slowly climbs the dark air of the dale. As the path reaches the end of the dale a flat area of ground on the right-hand side, close by the clapper bridge, is all that remains of a fisherman's cottage, which stood here until it was demolished in the 1950s. A number of photographs that feature the old cottage suggest an idyllic scene, but the cold, dark and damp of the valley floor in winter, where sun never shines, would have made this a hard place to live.

Youlgrave is built on ground that rises to the north, and the houses and cottages are strung out along the south-facing hillside, following the

Grey heron

Slow worm

topography of the dale. Lead miners' cottages run along this rising slope and also down into the dale itself. The warm sheltered gardens, with their high retaining stone walls and the dale side below them, are home to large numbers of slow worms, which can be seen basking in spring and summer sunshine. Coldwell End is one of the few places where slow worms can be seen in the Peak District.

While the grander houses of the village are away from the dale and close to the church, the eighteenth and early nineteenth century dwellings of the poor, tiny terraced cottages, cling to the hillside with their garden plots running into and across the dale. This indicates how close the residents of Youlgrave were to their work down the mineshafts and to the Moatlow and Coldwell Commons where they once grazed their animals.

From the valley bottom, the cottages and houses of Coldwell End are barely visible to those who walk the dale, but the residents in their dale-side eyries can view the path and the river for much of the year, when the ash and sycamore are bare. This was the view that Anthony Wragg (Chris's second cousin) had as a child in Coldwell End, where he still lives:

'We grew up looking over the dale. We came out of the back door and looked across the dale. It was just there, we never thought about it. We used to cut down King Street to the river. We used to swim in the river every summer. There would be loads of kids down there, swimming and just enjoying ourselves. My mum or somebody would shout down the dale, "Come in it's tea time". So you would pack up all your stuff and come back home. We used to have different camps down there and we'd make a little fire. I had three brothers and a sister. There were a lot more kids up at Coldwell End in those days. There were eight of us in the Top End Gang. It was a smashing atmosphere really. In the evening we'd play cricket or football in the road because there was no traffic. The centre line was the wicket.'

Chris Wragg's family once lived on King Street, a path that leads into the dale:

'My Granny used to live down there … and my Uncle Enos was the last one who lived down there. You could set off on Main Street and it was cold and frosty and turn off down to my Grandma's and the difference in temperature was unbelievable. My dad said they used to bath outside in a tin bath on the step.

We used to keep hens down the dale. It was my job to feed them and put them out and shut them up morning and evening. Sometimes when I was feeding the hens at dusk this light thing comes flying over with its two eyes staring, just like a ghost. A barn owl hunting the dale – it's a scary thing to see at dusk. There was an open area (below Coldwell End) by the weir, where we used to find slow worms. We would turn over stones and if you found a slow worm you brought it home at times and kept it. But if you grabbed it by the tail, it shed its tail to get away.'

The steep climb up out of the valley to Youlgrave still sets hearts racing, but for past residents this daily exercise was increased by the burden of carrying water up to the village.

Above : Bradford Dale and beyond viewed from Coldwell End
Left : The western end of Youlgrave seen from the hill above Mawstone

Bringing Water to Youlgrave

The piped water that flows into our homes is a privilege that we are accustomed to thinking of as a necessity. In the developed world we enjoy this amenity without thinking about it, but 2.5 billion people in the world do not use improved sanitation and eight hundred million have no safe drinking water. According to World Health Organisation figures, 1.8 million people (mainly children) die each year from water-related diseases. The almost inconceivable hardships of people whose lives seem remote from ours are brought to our attention by charity fundraising efforts. But we do not need to look far to see close parallels in the living conditions of our forebears.

In the past, the dependence on wells, springs and rivers was absolute. In the early nineteenth century in Youlgrave, apart from a few neighbourhood wells in the village, the water was carried from the river up the stone steps of Bankside to Coldwell End or up Holywell Lane to the centre of the village. The continuous drudgery of carrying water fell to the women. The water itself, running through the limestone bedrock, was hard and did not lend itself to washing and laundry. Either rainwater was used for these jobs or the women had to travel even further to collect softer water from a stream that rose from a spring on the gritstone bedrock of the hillside at Mawstone, which lies to the south of Youlgrave.

In high summer, July and August, the fever months, it seems likely that the sickness and death of young children in Youlgrave was linked to the impurity of the river water. Low water levels in summer time and through drought periods would have caused greater levels of pollution and concentrations of bacteria. Drinking water direct from the river could be a hazardous business, especially in view of the effluent from Middleton draining into the river half a mile upstream.

Throughout Britain during the nineteenth century, the unsanitary conditions of both the burgeoning urban working classes and the rural poor were coming to the attention of social reformers and philanthropists. The Sanitary Reform Movement was started in the 1830s, aiming to improve the sanitary conditions of urban areas, and a *Report on the Sanitary Condition of the Labouring Population in Great Britain*, by Edwin Chadwick, published in 1842, led to the first Public Health Act of 1848. A link had been made between poverty, squalor and disease that eventually led to the establishment of Boards of Health and concerted efforts to clean water supplies and create safe drainage.

Before the wheels of public administration began to address the problems of the urban poor, the women of Youlgrave were galvanised into action to improve conditions for local people by founding the Friendly Society of Women in 1827. A wealthy local woman, Hannah Bowman, spearheaded a campaign to supply piped water in order to save the labours of the women and the lives of children in Youlgrave.

A clean water supply has been regarded through time as a fundamental requirement for a successful and thriving community. The visionary efforts of the women in Youlgrave made this a reality in 1829. Funds were raised (£275) for a pipe that was laid between the spring at Mawstone and the centre of the village, close to the Bull's Head Inn. A circular stone tower was erected to act as a cistern for the water. This collecting tank held 1,200 gallons of water. The tank has always been known as 'the Fountain', and its location 'Fountain Square'.

An overseer was employed to unlock the tap each day. The local people each paid a subscription of 6d per year for their water. The tank, emptied through the day, would recharge overnight. The supply of water to the village was a cause for celebration and this heralded the introduction of the first recorded dressing of the water tap at the Fountain in Youlgrave. Since then well dressing, or more strictly 'tap dressing', has become central to the traditions and character of Youlgrave.

Over time, the two-inch cast iron pipe began to corrode and leak, and the water supply become unreliable. Once again, in 1869 village people rallied round to raise funds for a new £400 pipeline. Each able-bodied man of the village had to contribute three days' labour or the equivalent price of that labour. The considerable cost of the venture was met partly by villagers and also by wealthy benefactors. This time the source of the supply was slightly further east in a spring rising in Bleakley Wood. Supply to the village added greatly to everyone's convenience as a mains pipe carried water to taps in six locations in the village, with a further four at Bradford. Some of the tap spots were close to where the old wells had been.

There were great celebrations for the second opening of Youlgrave's water supply. A ceremony was held at what is now Fountain Square on 27 July 1869 and the Matlock Brass Band led a parade of 400 children. A dinner for 300 was held in the new schoolroom, followed by a public tea *'with an immense number of people attending'*. For this occasion and on most subsequent years Youlgrave's Well Dressings have been placed at or close by the locations of these first water taps.

While community resourcefulness secured safe water supplies in many rural areas across Britain in the past, most domestic water supplies are now in the hands of big corporations. Few villages or towns can boast a water company that is owned and run by the community, but Youlgrave Waterworks continues a proud tradition of owning and managing its own water supply as it has done for the last 180 years. In Part 5 we will hear more of the challenges and achievements of Youlgrave Waterworks.

Left : Looking east from the clapper bridge
Right : Looking west up the dale from the clapper bridge

The gardens of Bankside circa 1900 (photo supplied by Gordon Coupe)

Holywell or Holloway Lane

Holywell Lane was formerly Holloway Lane, indicating that this was probably an ancient thoroughfare – one of the old hollow ways. These were thoroughfares that were literally worn down into the ground by use over hundreds of years, thereby making the way 'hollow'. Another local name is 'Oliver Lane'.

The medieval clapper bridge that spans the river at the bottom of Holywell Lane punctuates the opening of Bradford Dale. Several paths meet here: Holywell Lane leads up into the village; steps lead up through Bankside to Coldwell End; a path rises south towards what is called 'Ow'd Mouth' and the way across the meadow follows the river along to Alport. The Old Mouth is an old lead mine, now visible as a cave opening by the path that leads south up out of the dale.

Bankside and Knocking Alley

Above the river at Bankside, various cottages face south into the dale along short terraces. Rather as the fishermen's cottages cling to the steep cliff sides of coastal communities, so these lead miners' cottages cling to the dale sides. In the past, terraced gardens rose steeply above the river alongside the path to Bankside. These have been recreated and worked on in recent years to provide carefully laid vegetable and orchard plots.

One terrace of cottages, Fowler's Row, was once known as 'Knocking Alley'. A row of nine miners' cottages stood at right-angles to Coldwell End leading towards the dale. Here women and children would work at 'dressing' the lead ore by hitting or 'knocking' large pieces of ore that were called 'bing' to remove waste or what are known as 'gangue' materials. This had to be done where there was a stone floor or paving and there was only one place that was suitable in the dale. As lead mining

Lucy Mead playing in the shallows 1996

Fisherman's cottage and clapper bridge circa 1900 (photo supplied by Gordon Coupe)

was the main industry in the area for 150 years, Knocking Alley would have been an important place. There were two other types of lead ore: 'peas' and 'smithems'. Hammers were used to break ('knock') ore into pea-sized pieces that were then sieved in water. The heavy lead ore sank and the worthless lighter rock was discarded. Once this initial work was done, the ore was then 'buddled' in a long trough or gutter known as a 'launder' from which waste materials were skimmed off and discarded. Smithems were the very small pieces of lead rendered by this process. Many people in Youlgrave still refer to house gutters as 'launders'. [18]

Much of the lead ore was processed close to the mines and the leavings were often picked over and sorted later on by poor people who were able to make a small living from what they could extract from the spoil heaps along the lead rakes.

The shallow waters at the opening of the dale have provided a playground for children of the village and for visitors for generations. The ford across the river by the clapper bridge makes for excellent paddling. This part of the river with its relatively easy access has also been used for years by well dressers. In the two weeks prior to Well Dressing (which always falls close to midsummer) the timber frames and boards of the well dressings are brought to soak in the river by well dressers assisted by a local farmer with his tractor and trailer. The boards are soaked so that the clay, which is the basis for the well dressings, retains moisture thus prolonging the life of the petals, leaves and mosses used in the designs.

[18] Behind the Primitive Methodist Chapel is an area called Westcroft. This name is believed to be a corruption of 'wash croft', this being a place in which lead was washed or 'laundered' (information from Gordon Coupe). A patch of ground has been left bare owing to the poisoning or 'bellanding' of the ground through years of lead processing. See footnote on belland on page 88.

Youlgrave Well or 'Tap' Dressing

Despite a higher-than-average rainfall in this area, the White Peak is a dry place. Water does not stay on the surface of the ground but it vanishes, even after heavy rainfall, and in the summer rivers dry out. In the same way, quite suddenly, water can gush from the mouth of a cave (as it does at the head of Lathkill Dale) or thread down from a dale side or bubble up into the ground or through a streambed. There is a sense here of the mysterious and unseen movement and direction of water in the unknowable underground environment. This is a place where no one has ever taken water for granted and this may help to explain why Derbyshire has long upheld the unique custom of decorating its water sources.

The connection between water and spirituality runs deep through many religions and in the pre-Christian era our Celtic forbears worshipped the spirits they believed inhabited the natural world. It is known that springs and wells were sites of special significance and that spirits were thought to dwell in the places where water flowed.

The Romans also worshipped gods associated with water and paid tribute to them. It is a human instinct to celebrate water sources, but both the

Romans and early Christians regarded the Ancient Britons' worship of springs and wells as sacrilegious and exercised their power by imposing their own belief systems and forms of worship. The Council of Arles (an early representative meeting of Christian bishops in the western Roman Empire) in 452 forbade anyone from worshipping trees, stones or springs. Pagan rituals of decorating water sources were, no doubt, the first well dressings, but the old religions were stamped out by both Roman and later Christian rulers. Many wells and ancient springs now carry the names of saints or are known simply as 'holy wells'.

The Bubonic Plague or Black Death, the pandemic that spread from Asia through Europe killing thirty to sixty per cent of the population, wrought havoc as it spread from the ports and cities of the south into country areas. The height of the pandemic in Britain was from 1348 to 1349. It is said that the White Peak village of Tissington lost only one person to this disease, while elsewhere communities were devastated. The people of Tissington believed that the purity of their water supply had saved them. They then decorated their wells and springs to give thanks for their salvation. For this same village, high on the limestone plateau, the water supply was cause for celebration once more in 1615 when, during a drought lasting four months, their wells continued to supply them with water. This drought followed on from a severe winter that was recorded in Youlgrave's Parish records as a *Memoriall of the Great Snow*. The 1615 celebration is the first certain record of well dressing in Derbyshire, although the precise details of the history of this community art cannot be established.

Well dressing is likely to have had its origins in pre-Christian times but in the popular revival of the custom in the nineteenth century it was closely associated with church ritual and blessing, and biblical scenes were often depicted in the well dressing with quotes from scripture. This practice continues today and Youlgrave dressings have a mix of iconography ranging from biblical scenes to contemporary events, aspects of the local landscape, and reference to other religious or secular themes relating to water.

Left : Erecting the Holywell tap dressing in 2008
Right : Ground water bubbling up in Gratton Dale

'Water taken straight from the earth has a mysterious quality … This is the quality of sanctity. Whether or not we associate these sites with specific ancient deities (or their saintly equivalents) does, perhaps, for us today, make no great difference – they are places where the Spirit of water is experienced, through which a contact can be made between ourselves and the formative forces of the cosmos.'

Whelan and Taylor, *Yorkshire Holy Wells and Sacred Springs*, 1989

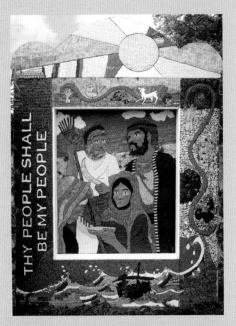

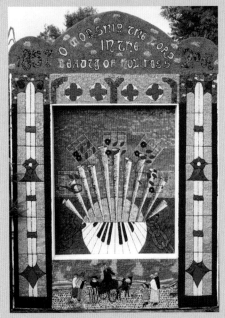

Tap dressings from Youlgrave 2006-7 and from Middleton 2012

The Fountain in Youlgrave was first decorated to celebrate the arrival of piped water to the village in 1829. When the water supply was restored and piped to the village in 1869 the Fountain was dressed and so began an almost unbroken annual tradition of well dressing in Youlgrave. The precise location of each of the five well dressings has shifted slightly down the years, but does roughly correspond to the original sites of some of the taps that brought water into the village in 1869. They are at Coldwell End, Bankside, Holywell Lane, Fountain Square, and at All Saints Church.

'A typical screen comprises five large, shallow wooden trays, which when elevated are at least 9 ft by 7 ft. The trays are laid flat on trestles, then filled with clay and smoothed to an even surface onto which the lines of the design are imprinted from paper templates.

When these have been delineated in black knitting wool, natural materials such as moss, parsley, and flower petals are pressed into the clay to create a picture (often biblical) surrounded by an ornate border with a theme or text (always biblical) below. Each well has its own regular designer and team of well dressers, who work from Monday to Friday in order to have the screen completed and erected early on Saturday, prior to the ceremony of Blessing the Wells in the afternoon. It will remain on display for five complete days before being dismantled the following Friday.

Well dressing is a skilful and painstaking task, especially as single flower petals must be laid precisely like tiles on a roof. The petals being delicate and perishable, they cannot be laid until Thursday at the earliest. So much concentration is required and teams have been known to work through Friday night. The designers prepare the artistry, direct the work and choose suitable materials. Garden flowers, particularly hydrangeas, are essential, but wildflowers such as buttercups are favoured where practicable. Collecting them is how most young well dressers begin their careers.

Tradition requires the screens to be on display at Midsummer Day (feast of St. John the Baptist) – or as near to it as possible.'

From the Youlgrave website: *www.youlgrave.com*

Middleton-by-Youlgrave has its own well dressing which takes place on the last week in May. This annual celebration was started in Middleton in 1977.

Top : Erecting the Fountain tap dressing in 2008
Above and right : Making the Coldwell End tap dressing in 2007

Brookleton

The meadow area between Holywell Lane and Bradford was once known as Brook-le-ton, which was almost certainly a Norman name. At Brookleton the character of the dale alters, the river valley opens out and the surrounding flood plain increases in area. This end of the dale has proved irresistible to visitors and locals for decades, a rural idyll that is enjoyed by crowds, who come to picnic here and play in the river on warm summer days. It is rare to find oneself alone in this place at any time of year between dawn and dusk.

'On Brookleton we dammed up the river and we used to swim in that. At carnival time they used to put a tree trunk across the dam and then had pillow fights. It was fantastic. You didn't know any other way of life, just living along the dale. We didn't have holidays. My Mum and Dad couldn't afford holidays. But I think I'd rather be on the dale than go to Blackpool personally. The dale was a big part of my life, especially when I was a kid. In our early teens we would keep going down, because all the girls used to go down there swimming. It was just a lovely place to play in.'

Anthony Wragg

People, dogs and cattle, sometimes sheep, mingle along this stretch of the river, making it hard for the wildlife that should thrive here to tolerate this otherwise ideal habitat. At quieter times grey wagtails fly low over the water and alight on rocks in the stream in their search for insects. Dippers also work this stretch of water and in the autumn kingfishers may streak through in a dazzling moment of cobalt blue. Many small birds take shelter in the thorn trees on both sides of the dale and they can be seen bathing in the river and drying themselves in a little bush that forms a kind of bird 'spa'. The hips and haws on the bushes along the river are valuable autumn food for blackbirds, long-tailed tits, song thrushes and our winter visitors, the fieldfares and redwings.

Where the river becomes shallow through the grasses of the meadow, it lightens the gloom of the deepening shadows of autumn and winter afternoons.

Kingfisher on a dried hogweed stem in November

Bradford

Mawstone Lane links Youlgrave to Elton via Gratton and crosses the river just before it turns north-west. It seems likely that before the construction of the road bridge this was the location of the 'broad ford' that gave both the river and dale their name. This part of Youlgrave is called Bradford and it is close to some of the numerous mine workings that were part of the Alport mining field. The lane called Stoneyside leads up from the river to the church. Its cottages and allotments face west up the dale. This was the miners' road up to their modest homes on the hillside.

Lillian Clark started life at Coldwell End in a lead miner's cottage. She moved away from Youlgrave when she married in the 1960s. She decided to return to the village in the 1980s to reconnect with her (estimate of) 260 relatives:

'We lived in Knocking Alley until I was four or five. There was a slop kitchen and one room downstairs and two little bedrooms upstairs and an earth toilet outside. I was about five when we moved down to the council houses in 1938. One of my earliest memories is of paddling in the river. We went down there to play all the time in the Parish watering hole where the cows used to be brought at Bradford Bridge. All the mothers used to come out and sit with us. They didn't let you go down and play by yourself.

When we were a bit older we'd walk further up the river wearing plimsolls. We'd fill a sauce bottle with powdered lemonade and take a bit of bread and lard, and we'd be gone all day. There was nothing you see, it was war-time. We'd go right up the dale and we'd walk up the fish ladders. We always took a jar for tiddlers but we were always told to put them back. All the men used to go fishing, pinching fish from the Duke. They'd put them in the bath then kill them for food.

My dad worked at Friden Brick Works from when he was fourteen years old. He did fifty years there. He used to walk up to Friden and do a twelve-hour shift and then walk back until he could afford to buy a bicycle.

We used to go swimming at the big bend in the river on the Coach Road. We either went there or the New Dam, but you had to be a good swimmer to go there. There was a lot of clemency during the war, but later they started fencing things in and getting more control.

On the Coach Road there were no trees in those days. You could see all the rocks. We used to go running on the rocks and we would get bunches of violets and toadflax. There was more sunshine on the dale. Up on the scree below Moatlow, there were mountain pansies and rock-roses. Now the trees have got a lot bigger, the leaf cover's got vast and everywhere is dark and damp, whereas once it was all open. All that scree on the hillside, that was gorgeous, golden sunshine reflecting down on to the river. It was more open, more uplifting really. I find the dale very depressing when I go. There are shadows now where there was dappled sunshine.

When we went for a walk on a Sunday, we might see a tree that had blown down or a limb that had broken off. We'd make a note of it (as we couldn't 'work' on Sunday), and sometimes we'd go back next day and it had already gone. You didn't tell anyone if you saw a tree down or they'd get up earlier than you and get it. You didn't see dead wood lying around. People were like a swarm of locusts picking it up. We would all go sticking and if anybody who'd got an old pram or pram wheels, they were made – you could get a load of twigs on a trolley or pram.'

The narrow stream of the Bradford meets the outflow water from the 'New Dam' that runs along a ditch through Hollow Farm. This narrow waterway is an important wildlife habitat and a place where the native white-clawed crayfish were able to survive through the drought that caused much of the River Bradford to dry out in 2011. Snipe have often been seen here in the past and kingfishers hunt here for small fry of the coarse fish that are washed down from the dam.

The New Dam

The so-called New Dam lies east of Bradford Dale and the wild creatures of the River Bradford exploit these linked habitats. The dam was built to harness water power for the first hydraulic engine to be installed in the Alport lead mining field by the great Cornish engineer and inventor Richard Trevithick, at the beginning of the nineteenth century *(see page 95)*. The dam is full of fish including carp, roach and perch and is popular with coarse fishermen who can obtain day permits from the owners at Hollow Farm.

As the only open stretch of standing water for many miles around, it is a valuable wildlife habitat. The dam itself is fed by Bleakley Dike, the stream that runs from a spring rising below Harthill Moor that has been the principal water source for Youlgrave since 1869. The marshy ground

Top left : Grey wagtail in October
Above : A cow from Hollow Farm (no longer a dairy farm) enjoying the waters of the New Dam
Right : Grey heron in the New Dam

around Bleakley Dike at the southern end of the dam supports a number of visiting waders such as lapwing, curlew and snipe. Cormorants also have been seen here. Canada and greylag geese, and grey heron, are here much of the time. Even a little egret and an osprey have been sighted. Other waterfowl and ducks such as tufted duck, mandarin, goosander, shoveler and widgeon have visited the dam, and mallard are regulars, together with coots and moorhens.

This continues to be an important spawning ground for toads. In March or early April huge numbers can be seen along the lanes, tracks and paths that lead to the New Dam and all too often they get killed by passing traffic.

Sadly, most of our visiting waders such as lapwing and curlew now pass through, whereas only twenty years ago they stayed to nest in sizeable numbers, raising their young in the quieter and more secluded fields around Youlgrave and Middleton. Here, as in much of the rest of the White Peak, the waders have now deserted the intensively farmed pastures to breed on the moors and moorland fringes of the Dark Peak.

Left : New Dam in winter
Above : Common toad
Top right : Kingfisher in the nature reserve near Alport
Far right : Packhorse bridge along the Coach Road

Bradford to Alport

The track that follows the stream along to Alport is called the Coach Road, once a favourite carriage route of former Dukes of Rutland.

The narrow stream runs through dense reeds where water voles were once a common sight. Various fence posts and trees provide kingfishers with perches along the way.

A path high on the rim of the valley on the village side of the stream gives a view of the river valley ahead and the wider landscape. From here, Harthill Castle Ring and Robin Hood's Stride dominate the skyline to the south.

Outcrops of bright pale reef-knoll limestone glow even on a gloomy day and lend dynamism and a distinctive atmosphere to the little valley that leads to Alport. A packhorse bridge crosses the stream by the first limestone crag and leads onto a walled track that rises up the hill towards the church. Along the steep bank on the east side of the stream there are various small caves and rock shelters that have provided local children with hideouts over generations. In the narrow flood plain along the Coach Road a considerable area of raised ground covers old lead mining shafts and spoil heaps. It is thought that these mines date back to the seventeenth century.

There are other spoil heaps in this part of the dale which are host to a rich variety of plant species associated with old lead works, including spring sandwort (known locally as 'leadwort') and alpine pennycress. Another rarity which grows here is maiden pink, and on the north dale side other unusual plants grow, including knotted clover, field madder and hoary cinquefoil. Dark mullein and musk mallow are also found here, as well as species more common to the limestone pastures such as yarrow and lady's bedstraw.[19]

A footpath rises steeply from the Coach Road and leads onto the level ground near Hollow Farm that was at the heart of the Alport mining field. This path passes through lead rakes and a dry-stone wall 'beehive' tops an old mineshaft.[20] When the mines were abandoned the waste material left behind (that had traces of zinc and lead in it) allowed unusual metal-tolerant (metallophyte) plant species to establish. While there are only two true metallophyte species in the White Peak (alpine pennycress and spring sandwort), a host of other plants such as harebells, birdsfoot trefoil, helianthemum, and mountain pansy flourish on the exposed hillocks.

Nowadays these paths and tracks provide locals and visitors with peaceful circuits to exercise themselves and their dogs but these same paths were once the routes to and from the numerous mineshafts that lie beneath these tranquil wooded banks and fields.

The open, unfenced grazing comes to an end, and a gate opens onto a meadow where the path is at a distance from the river. A small nature reserve alongside the river has been fenced off, securing an important refuge for wildlife. The narrow channel has a wall running along its west bank, but reeds and small trees have grown, allowing the formation of small meanders through the developing marshy areas. This is ideal habitat for many river creatures, and it appears that this may be the last stronghold of water voles along the Bradford. The kingfisher hunts here, and during the nesting season, when the birds have mainly retreated to the quieter sections of the river downstream, they sometimes venture here to fish.

Top left : Flowers on the lead rakes at Hollow Farm
Left : Nature reserve near Alport

[19] Information from Rhodri Thomas PDNPA. [20] Beehives are stone-built structures that covered a shaft opening and provided ventilation to the mine, while protecting stock and people from falling in.

Rhienstor Rock

The largest of the limestone crags along the Coach Road is currently named in OS maps Rhienstor Rock. Another spelling commonly used for the crag is Raenstor – an abbreviation of Raven's Tor. This twenty-four-metre high reef-knoll has been classified as a Regionally Important Geological Site (RIGS). On close examination characteristic brachiopod fauna (fossilised bivalved shellfish) can be seen (*see Appendix 1*). The date 1753 is carved into the rock, which most likely commemorates an extension of the Alport Sough (one of the many drainage tunnels driven to drain the lead mines).

The name Raenstor Rock tells us that this high cliff was once the haunt of ravens. These iconic birds were persecuted to such an extent that they were extinct in this area until relatively recently. Youlgrave's Parish Records carry an extensive archive of the price paid by the parish for the death of many species of birds and animals. The pennies paid to the killers of 'vermin' were valuable to impoverished country people. In 1666 Youlgrave Churchwardens paid 8d for two dead ravens and a shilling for another four. There was wholesale persecution of ravens in much of upland Derbyshire until well into the last century. Thankfully ravens have made a great recovery and now breed close to Elton and in Lathkill Dale. They are often to be seen flying above the dale, their complex language of barks, croaks and calls echoing along the valley.

The stream meanders close to the Coach Road at Raenstor Rock, becoming shallow before it flows under the track at Raenstor Cottage. The Coach Road then joins the road to Youlgrave at the bottom of Alport Hill. The very last stretch of the river Bradford flows in almost perpetual shade, under the hill on its eastern bank.

Above : Raven
Right : Rhienstor or Raenstor Rock near Alport

The Confluence

The clear waters of the River Lathkill flow in to the Bradford from the north and join it at Alport. Few people – locals or visitors – can resist looking into these waters from both sides of the main road bridge. There is great contrast to be seen on each side of the bridge. The gentle flow over the shallow weirs on the north side of the bridge contrasts with the sharp drop in levels flowing under the bridge towards the confluence. When in full flood, this is the place to view the torrent that pounds over and around the rocky fall. In winter, the river makes big incursions into the vegetable patch of Monks Hall. Forlorn brussels sprouts and leeks are sometimes awash with the floodwaters.

Alport is famed for its tufa, assessed by a RIGS survey in 1992 as being the thickest tufa deposit in Derbyshire (nine metres at its thickest). Tufa is a porous rock formed as a deposit from streams or springs. Deposits build on organic materials such as moss, roots, branches or vegetation. The calcium-rich accretions gradually, over time, incorporate the plant materials into the rock. The grass around parts of Alport is said to be 'crunchy'. The River Lathkill flows fast over ridged deposits of tufa, creating the turbulence below the bridge. There are small caves within the tufa. The Victorians were very fond of tufa as a garden feature, and it was extracted here for that purpose.

Left : River Lathkill flows past Monks Hall at Alport
Below : Footbridge at Alport

Alport Flour Mill

The stretch of river that runs downstream from the confluence with the Lathkill is sometimes called the Daykin and it meets the River Wye near Picory Corner. A small stone footbridge spans the river just below the confluence and was formerly a private bridge leading to Monks Hall. The actual confluence of the rivers is hard to see, as it is just beyond the path or view from the main road bridge, but an idea of the power of the joint force of these two rivers can be gained by standing on the footbridge downstream or by looking at Alport weir beside the corn mill, from the old bridge that crosses to Elton.

The combined force of the Bradford and Lathkill pounds over the weir that once powered the beautiful Alport Flour Mill. Now the old mill building houses water-powered turbines that generate electricity that feeds the National Grid when river flow is strong enough. Much of Alport belongs to Haddon Estate, which installed the power plant in July 2011. Hydroelectric power generated by the river now provides a sustainable source of energy.

The river flows along a private stretch of land between Alport and Hawley's Bridge. Travellers along the road to Youlgrave can see the weirs and pools through the trees. This is a popular river for fishermen, who can fish for trout undisturbed. The valley through which this river flows was once the throbbing centre of the Alport lead processing operation, with several lead smelting cupolas and a giant chimney built into the hillside. All that is now evident of this operation are the ruins of stone buildings and a chimney, barely visible through the dense woodland that has grown up along the valley.

At Hawley's Bridge, the river flows through flooded, marshy ground, which rarely drains. The continuous flooding of this area is due to blocked and broken soughs from the days of lead mining. Herons are often seen fishing here. The river then meanders through pastures that form the flood plain of the River Wye and it meets the Wye close to Picory Corner. The Wye then flows east to meet the south-flowing River Derwent at the confluence just south of Rowsley.

River Lathkill viewed from the road bridge at Alport

Alport and the Portway

Alport is at the end of our journey through the past along the river. Now a tranquil hamlet, its cottages and larger houses with their garden plots fill the spaces made by the converging rivers.

Alport was a very important place in the past, for two reasons. It derives its name from the Portway, the ancient track or route through Derbyshire, which passed through the village. The proximity of the Portway to Alport, Youlgrave and Middleton would have been vital in terms of the communication, trade and transport that sustained these communities from the earliest times.

The other reason for its fame was that the Alport lead mining field was one of the most heavily worked mining areas in the Peak District. It was also a centre for lead processing. Part 3 focusses on the importance of lead mining in the past and its impact on our rivers and water supplies today.

Portway is an Old English word, *port-weg*, that the Anglo-Saxons used for an important road or way that was already in use before their arrival. Wirksworth, Bakewell (*Badecan Wiellon*) and Ashbourne (*Aescforda*) were all Saxon settlements but the Portway was, as we have seen, most likely used by travellers from the Bronze Age and earlier.

The word *port* referred to a market, and this ancient trading route linked up people and their products until well into the eighteenth century when goods were conveyed across the Peak District on packhorses. *Auld* meant old and so it is likely that *Aulport* was known as a trading centre or market long before it attained its market charter in the fourteenth century. There are two other Alports in Derbyshire, one high in the Dark Peak (Alport Castles) and Alport Hill close to Wirksworth. All three derive their name from their proximity to the Portway.

The ancient track followed ridges and high places, thereby keeping travellers safe from the perils of the thickly forested and marshy river valleys. The Portway passed through Alport in a north–south direction,

crossing the river by way of an ancient ford that was situated between Monks Hall and the corn mill. The precise route in to Alport is uncertain, but according to Dodd and Dodd the variety of species in the hedges on the lane from Elton to Alport indicates that this was an ancient route dating at least back to the Middle Ages.

The Portway continued to be an important trade and communication route for many hundreds of years despite the perils that the river presented to travellers before the bridges and later turnpike roads were built. The route was heavily used by packhorse trains and other traffic well into the eighteenth century. At that time there was no road into the hamlet from the east downstream. Fording the river at Alport was clearly a hazardous business when it was swollen. In 1718 a complaint was made to the Derbyshire Sessions that urged the desperate need for a bridge at Alport.

Top left : Entrance to Dark Lane and the old Portway route
Top right : The route of the Portway through Alport along Joules Lane

'Great gangs of London Carriers as well as drifts of malt-horses and other carriers and passengers goe this ancient waye, which lies in a hollow frequently over-flowed by the swollen stream. Heavy rains have so scoured out the channel as to render the ford impassable for as long as 8 or 10 days, whilst at all times carriers with loaden horses and passengers cannot pass the saide road without great danger of being cast away.'

While the Sessions agreed to this demand and directed the building of a horse bridge, Alport had to wait another eighty years before the present bridge over the river above the corn mill was constructed in 1800. This wider bridge was able to carry wagons and coaches.

Above : Tufa Rock, Alport   **Right** : Track to the lime kilns and corn mill at Alport

The Portway goes north from Alport up a steep track called Dark Lane, passing by what locals call 'Tufa Rock' (an unusual crag of tufa). The caves here were used to shelter animals and also as a shelter for wagons, the remains of which can still be seen. Dark Lane climbs the hill to the wide plateau of Haddon Fields which was once a scene of battle between local lead miners and armed horseman engaged by the Duke of Rutland *(see page 82).*

You can follow the path used by travellers over centuries up Dark Lane, across the plateau to 'Two Trees', turn right along the lane then find the way that leads north round Bakewell to Ashford. You would be following in the footsteps of Bronze Age traders, pilgrims, Saxon traders and jaggers with their trains of mules and horses that carried wool, salt, lead or malt across the hills and dales of the Peak District for hundreds of years.[21]

[21] From the Middle Ages until the nineteenth century packhorses and packmules were the principal means of transporting goods across the Peak District as they were able to cope with the rough terrain. 'Jagger' was the name given to the man in charge of the animals and their loads. The name occurs in a number of Derbyshire locations and may relate to a breed of horses – German Jaegers – that were favoured in this area.

… The former sacred ways,
The footpaths, sunlit bridleways, lovers' lanes
… Delicate arteries, once worn in by thought

Heathcote Williams, *Autogeddon*, 1991

Part 3
The Impact of Lead Mining

'All this country is hollow. Could you strike it with some gigantic hammer it would boom like a drum.'

Sir Arthur Conan Doyle, *Tales of Terror and Mystery*, 1922

View from above Mawstone across the Alport mining field to the Eastern Moors.

There are over fifty different versions of the name for Youlgrave, but it is generally considered that the name links the place to lead mining from long ago. 'Groove' is an ancient name (probably Old English) for a lead mine and this was an 'Auldgroove'. Lead mining had gone on here for centuries and has had a massive impact on the landscape, the rivers and the people.

Any visitor walking in the White Peak using an Ordnance Survey map will soon become familiar with the ubiquitous Shafts (dis) (1:25 000) or Mines (dis) (1:50 000). These features pepper the landscape and reveal the extent to which lead mining governed the lives and livelihoods of those who lived in the White Peak in the past. Some small workings scattered about in fields, and very often remote from any dwellings, represent the small-scale enterprises of individual miners who scratched and dug a living for themselves out of the limestone bedrock. Others were much greater concerns. For example the Cow Close Mine at Elton extracted forty thousand pounds' worth of lead ore each year through the 1740s and 1750s. In today's terms this was a multi-million pound industry, with only patches of disturbed ground to show for it now. The ancient industry of lead mining is what shaped the fortunes of the Derbyshire Dales in the past and some might say influences the character of its communities and its people even today.

Left : St Mary's and All Saints Church Youlgrave built with the aid of wealth made from lead mining
Right : Old mine entrance in the dale below Youlgrave

The ore from which lead is extracted in the White Peak is galena (lead sulphide) and it occurs in the mineral veins that run through the limestone. Methods of extraction depended heavily on the ways in which the minerals were contained within the rock and there were names given to different kinds of veins and the minerals associated with them *(see Appendix 2)*. The name most familiar to residents and visitors to the White Peak is 'rakes', which are major veins, but the term is commonly used to describe any lead veins.

The mineral veins were not packed out with lead ore. Galena was typically about five per cent of vein contents.[1] The old lead miners regarded other minerals that lay in the veins along with the lead ore as waste. These were left underground if possible, or in mounds that are characteristic of the orefield landscape. Today these minerals (barytes, calcite and fluorspar) constitute the mineral wealth of the Derbyshire Dales.

History of Lead Mining in the White Peak

We know that the Romans mined for lead in Derbyshire, but before the Roman occupation early Britons were extracting lead from the North Pennines and they probably did so in the Peak District as well. While the Romans had the capability to mine from underground, all evidence points to their working along exposed lead veins using opencast methods.

A soft and malleable, dense material, impervious to the effects of water, lead has made an invaluable contribution to the development of building technology from Roman times. It has made channels for water as lead piping and guttering and it has been used to seal roofs and windows, creating watertight habitation for those who could afford it. Some say that the Romans, the inventors of plumbing, actually poisoned themselves with their piped water systems.

Medieval builders used it extensively in their stone castles, churches and great houses. Later uses included musket balls and lead shot. Today lead is used in batteries and to seal radiation treatment areas in hospitals.

Both the Saxons and Danes mined for lead. We can see the value of lead mines to the early church in the large rent payments made by Repton Abbey (which owned the Wirksworth mines in the ninth century) to Christ Church Canterbury *(Ford and Rieuwerts)*. The Danish army destroyed Repton Abbey in 874 and the lead mines of Wirksworth became the property of the Danish King Ceolwulf. This historical takeover eventually led to many of the orefields of the Peak District becoming what is called the 'King's Field' (now Queen's Field). This means that a proportion of lead ore mined within the King's/Queen's Field must be given to the Crown as a 'duty'. The Duchy of Lancaster still owns mineral duties within the areas defined as the Queen's Field.

[1] Some minerals associated with Galena were oxidised to form carbonates. These were used, in the case of lead carbonate, to make paint; and zinc carbonate for paint, brass making and medicinally as calamine (a skin balm and treatment for digestive complaints).

The Barmote Courts

In 1288 Edward I ordered an inquisition (enquiry) into the practice of lead mining in the Peak District. As a result of this the orefield was divided into different areas for administrative purposes, the High Peak and Low Peak being the principal ones in the King's/Queen's Field. Within these areas, the orefields were divided further into what are called 'liberties' and these roughly correspond to parish boundaries. The administration of a complex system of entitlements, duties and laws led to the establishment of the oldest industrial courts in the world, the Barmote (or Barmoot) Courts. While the peculiarities and particulars of lead mining law are beyond the scope of this book, it is interesting to note that anyone could search for lead on any land in the King's/Queen's Field apart from churchyards, highways, gardens and orchards. An individual could make a claim on a lead vein and start to mine it, once they had applied to the Barmaster to have it 'freed'. They then had to pay for the right to mine the lead with a certain quantity of ore measured by a 'freeing dish'.[2]

Once this was paid, they were allowed to work two measures called 'meers'. The third meer was called the Lord's Meer and belonged to whoever owned the mineral duties. The length of the meer varied in different areas but was generally around thirty yards. Duties consisted of the payment of a proportion of the lead ore that was mined to whoever owned the liberty. If a vein was not worked properly or to the satisfaction of the Barmaster, it could be 'nicked' by another miner.

Slightly different laws applied outside of the King's/Queen's Field and, in these private liberties, 'duties' were paid to individuals such as the Duke of Devonshire or the Earl (later the Duke) of Rutland.

In the seventeenth century battles took place on Haddon Fields in which armed '*military forces, mounted gentry and yeoman*' attacked lead miners who were trying to defend their rights against the unusually harsh restrictions and duties exacted by the Earl of Rutland.[3]

Left : Haddon Hall with Haddon Fields to the left and beyond

Above : 'Nicking' the Bacon Close Mine, Youlgrave, with the Barmaster second from right, circa 1920 (photo from Lyn Willies's collection)

Right : Dickie Bird explores a coffin level of Founterabbey Sough in Ball Eye Mine 1960 (photograph by Hilary Bird)

[2] A 'freeing dish' held about 65 lbs of ore. A standard dish presented to the Low Peak miners by Henry VIII in 1513 is kept at the Moot Hall in Wirksworth. [3] Ford and Rieuwerts, 2000. [4] 'T'owd man' was the name given to the old miners from previous times, or their ghosts. It was also the name given to waste left underground or places worked by miners in the past.

A Hard Life

Mining in the seventeenth century was a hazardous business and sometimes involved the setting of fires to fracture the limestone. Gunpowder was often used to open up new veins. But, largely speaking, from the Middle Ages until the eighteenth century the basic tools of the lead miner were a hammer and pick. The wielding of these tools produced what are called 'coffin levels', where the miners slowly drove their way through the limestone armed only with a pick and hammer, with the pick struck sideways-on through its metal shaft. The progress made in these handpicked levels was around two to three inches, or five centimetres, in a day.

The customs and practice of lead mining in Derbyshire have, from the earliest times, encouraged individual enterprise in this most gruelling and testing occupation. The perilous descent deep into the ground was driven by poverty and need, but also by the prospect of an honest living made from toil and personal endeavour. While an individual might 'strike lucky' with a rich lead vein, this was hardly like gold prospecting. The miners' rewards were limited and any glance at the housing stock of villages such as Youlgrave, Elton, Bonsall and Monyash reveals the great divide between those that mined for lead in the eighteenth and nineteenth centuries and those that were able to profit by selling it.

During the seventeenth century, lead merchants, smelters, and other investors began to buy up and expand mines. Gradually, more men were employed by mine owners, as the larger mines required greater levels of capital investment for drainage, installation of pumps, and ventilation systems. But at the same time small mines continued to be worked in the old ways, by miners on their own or in partnerships as miner-shareholders. A lot of miners were also farmers, or farm labourers, who couldn't make a living from just one of these occupations. The lone operators carried on working, using primitive methods, into the twentieth century.

In the early eighteenth century Daniel Defoe was particularly struck by the drama and peculiarities of 'T'owd man' emerging from the ground in the desolate open country of the limestone uplands.[4]

'We went ... to a valley on the side of a rising hill, where there were several grooves, (for so they call the mouth of the shaft or pit by which they go down into a lead mine) ... we were surprised with seeing a hand, and then an arm, and quickly after a head, thrust up out of the very groove we were looking at. Immediately we rode closer up to the place, where we saw the poor wretch working and heaving himself up gradually ... When this subterranean creature was come quite out, with all his furniture about him, he afforded us a new matter of wonder. The man was a most uncouth spectacle; he was clothed all in leather, had a cap of the same without a brim, some tools in a little basket which he drew up with him ... He was lean as a skeleton, pale as a corpse, his hair and beard a deep black; what little flesh he had was lank, and, as we thought something of the colour of the lead itself.'

Daniel Defoe, *A Tour Thro' the Whole Island of Great Britain*, Vol 2, 1724

Old lead workings at Moatlow

In the eighteenth century, a period in which the economy of Britain was expanding through slavery, industry, trade and commerce, a new mercantile class emerged. This new social class had the wealth to build fine houses and prompted an expansion of the domestic building trade. While in Bristol, Manchester and Liverpool much of the new money came from the slave trade and slave-produced cotton and sugar, here in Derbyshire it was mainly the lead mine owners, merchants, dealers and smelters who had the fine new stone houses built in the eighteenth century, which you can see in Wirksworth, Winster and other Dales towns and villages. The building boom in its turn served to keep the market for lead buoyant, so to speak, during the heyday of the industry from 1700 to 1750.

The lead industry of Derbyshire's principal orefield, which extended from Castleton in the north to Wirksworth in the south, was of international importance. Britain was Europe's main source of lead, and the Peak District was the most productive lead mining area. Ingots of lead – generally referred to as 'pigs' – were taken from here, mainly via Hull, across the sea. Lead ingots that probably came from Derbyshire have been found in Brittany (from a Roman vessel), on the Hollandia, wrecked off the Scillies in 1743, and off the coast of South Africa.[5]

Lead Smelting

The production of lead pigs by smelting most often took place outside the orefields of the White Peak. One of the notable exceptions was the large smelting operation at Alport that was a centre for considerable innovation in the nineteenth century.

There are numerous 'Bole Hills' dotted around Derbyshire and South Yorkshire that mark the sites of medieval smelting furnaces. In South Yorkshire some of these 'Bole Hills' were furnaces for smelting iron but the Derbyshire ones were, almost without exception, for lead processing. They were most often situated on high west-facing hills, exploiting the prevailing westerly winds to keep high temperatures maintained in the 'bole' and to carry the noxious fumes across the open moorland. On Beeley Moor there were many small, probably medieval, smelting boles. On the wooded scarp below the moors at Fallinge Edge, Smelting Wood and Burnt Wood are readily identified as former sites for lead smelting, but sites have been found dotted all along the Eastern Moors.

The hearths made on the hillsides were built with low stone walls and the moulten lead trickled into a basin from which pigs could be cast. The resulting 'slag' was sometimes re-fired at a higher temperature with charcoal to extract more lead. The sites were close to woods to fuel the fires and close to packhorse routes, so that the crudely made ingots could be carried further along on the trade routes. The main markets were Hull, Bawtry and London. Sometimes the pigs were taken to Chesterfield, which was a centre for lead trading, and to Sheffield, but Hull was one of the most important destinations for lead from the Middle Ages onwards.

Fallinge Edge viewed from Youlgrave

[5] Willies, 1990.

Froggatt Edge: throughout the history of lead mining, much of the smelting took place along the gritstone edges of the Eastern Moors

After the Middle Ages the smelting operations got bigger '... *boles appeared to have been much larger ... some six metres across, utilising whole trees for fuel, placed within three walls, the fourth side open to the wind.*'[6]

The complex chemistry of lead smelting depended for its success as much on the skills and efforts of the smelters and labourers as it did on the refinements in technology that developed over time. The early wind-blown smelting boles were replaced by hearths, fired by artificial blast from bellows powered by water.[7]

Streams all over Derbyshire were harnessed to power small smelting operations. It was the lead miners' right to smelt their own ore and many small operators exercised this right in the sixteenth and seventeenth centuries. But as the industry grew at the beginning of the eighteenth century it became more usual for miners to sell their ore to agents, who were often smelters. The smelting operations got bigger with greater concentration of capital and thus facilities. The fuel used in the big ore hearths was referred to as 'white coal' (kiln-dried wood chips). Enormous quantities of fuel were needed for each smelting operation.

In 1735 a new system of smelting was introduced into Derbyshire by the London Lead Company and by two local operators, Twigg and Bagshawe. New coal-fired reverberatory cupola furnaces *(see Appendix 4)* had been developed in the previous century, but the first to operate in Derbyshire was in Ashover, at Bowers Mill. Cupolas could yield around sixty-three per cent lead as against the more usual fifty per cent yield from the traditional hearth furnaces, and they sped up the smelting process. They required tall chimneys to supply the draught, such as the one that can still be seen at the well-known and extensive site at Stonedge, high on the moor's edge near Chesterfield. This square stack is the oldest industrial chimney in the world.

One of the aims of condensing fume through long flues was to reduce the amount of toxic material (belland) released onto surrounding land and stock.[8]

Slag contained valuable material that was often smelted again in a hearth,

which would operate alongside the cupola smelting furnaces. The slag mills were water-powered and so the newer smelting operations were often located near to a stream. By the middle of the nineteenth century Alport had become a major centre for both mining and smelting lead.

Alport Smelting Mills circa1860 (photo from Derbyshire Record Office)

Smelting Lead in Alport

Alport Lead Smelt Mill was situated downstream from Alport Flour Mill. Messrs. Barker and Rose established the business in 1847, hoping to make capital out of lead extracted from local mines. The Barker family were major players and had '*connections with and kept accounts of approximately a quarter to a third of the entire lead production of the Peak from 1730 to 1875.*'[9]

This was a considerable enterprise engaging all of the technological advances of the day. Its complex condensing flue system was state of the art. The main flue ran horizontally through the hillside along a double-

[6] Willies,1990. [7] The first furnaces to be blown by bellows were developed in the middle of the sixteenth century, by Humphrey and Burchard. The two men were in contention over the patents for their different furnaces. William Humphrey had a smelting mill built on the River Sheaf at Beauchief while Burchard's water-powered bellows worked his furnace in Duffield. Rieuwerts p30. The technologies devised by these two men were not improved upon in Derbyshire until well into the eighteenth century. [8] Belland is the fine dust of lead particles produced in dressing ore which could poison animals grazing in affected land or by drinking contaminated water (so an animal was said to be "bellanded"). Belland also refers to the spread of toxic material given off in the fume from smelting. Inhalation of fume was one of the hazards of the lead smelter. [9] Willies, 1983. [10] Percy, 1870 p240, see Willies, 1990 p7.

'The first shift began at 3 am on Monday till 8 or 9 am ... the smelters had to have the furnace heated to a certain pitch before the ore was put in ... For nearly forty years the Needhams' door could never be locked – her brother went to liberate (take over from) her father. The flues were cleaned out twice a year and when cleaning, the men had to have nose and mouth covered, and keep special clothes ... At dinner times on those occasions all was spoon-meat, broth or Irish Stew or a posset in winter, because they might not touch the food with their hands ... Fanny, as a child, used to take down eight cans of dinners at once, being hooked on to a stick about 2 feet long ... and she had to keep her distance. The cleaning went on from Monday till Friday, twice a year.

There were three kilns burning and a wagon and carts took the lead to Sheffield.'

Fanny was employed as a child in grinding and washing ore together with another girl. It is a wonder that, surrounded by so much toxic material, she survived well into her eighties.

looped passageway. The round chimneystack can still be seen through the trees high on the hillside north of the River Lathkill *(see above)*.

The site had two reverberatory smelting furnaces and a slag hearth. The Alport complex had, according to a contemporary commentator, the fastest smelting time of any of the lead works in Derbyshire in its period, taking just four to five hours. In the eighteenth century, cupola smelting had taken around twelve hours.[10]

Just as this smelting operation was established, Derbyshire lead mining and smelting was fast declining. The costs of 'unwatering' the mines made extraction unprofitable, lead prices were falling and so was demand. The business was sold in 1875, but did not function again after 1874, and in the 1890s Alport Lead Smelt Mill was closed for good.

Miss Fanny Thornhill Needham (born in 1847) was one of the oldest inhabitants of Alport. Her father worked for nearly forty years at the cupola lead works. Members of the Youlgrave Women's Institute recorded the following account in 1931:

Ruins of Alport Smelting Mills circa1900 (photo from Lyn Willies's collection)

Alport Mining Field

The tranquil winding of the River Bradford along the Coach Road from Mawstone Lane to the quaint hamlet of Alport belies the busy, noisy and polluted atmosphere of the past. Alport mining field was once one of the most intensively worked lead mining areas of the Peak District and consequently of Britain.

All the lead veins of the Alport mining area were private liberties (that is, outside the King's/Queen's Field). These are Haddon, Hartle (Harthill), Stanton and Youlgrave.

Fields, woods, trackways, spoil heaps and farm buildings are the only markers now of the complex system of mineshafts, underground drainage systems, soughs, flues and chimneys that operated here at the height of the mining bonanza in the eighteenth and nineteenth centuries. Hollow Farm was once a mining engineer's house and various field barns once had a dual use for both farming and mining equipment storage. There is even an explosives store close by Millfield Farm. The centre for operations of the Alport Mining Company was Broadmeadow Counting House and Smithy. These are now cottages with mine shafts below and close by. A few remnants of stone ruin now stand as a reminder of the clanking, smoking place that Alport once was in its heyday as a major centre for lead mining and smelting.

Left : The New Dam and Hollow Farm (centre) were at the heart of the Alport mining field
Below : Old mine workings are visble as raised ground alongside the River Bradford

'Unwatering' the Mines

The complex hydrogeology of the White Peak limestone presented lead miners with the greatest technical and practical difficulties as they went ever deeper into the ground. Even when working above the water table the lead mines were very wet, but as miners excavated below it the volumes of water made the work very difficult and dangerous.

The 'unwatering' of the Derbyshire lead mines required the greatest ingenuity and determination. It was a project that continued for three hundred years and cost a great deal of money and many lives. Some would say another cost has been irreparable damage to the natural flow of water both over and under the ground of the Derbyshire Dales. In the late eighteenth century the foremost technological advances of the age were brought to bear on the unwatering of the mines of Alport and solutions found that have consequences for the health of the River Bradford's flow and Youlgrave's water supply today.

The first attempts to unwater the mines involved rag and chain pumps (essentially buckets and winding gear). Later pumps were devised to raise the water, worked by manpower, horsepower and water wheels. The first steam engines devised by Thomas Newcomen were employed in Derbyshire in the eighteenth century to pump water from the mines. Three Newcomen engines were installed in the Alport mining field. But the greatest impact on the river systems of the White Peak came from the drainage channels dug by the Derbyshire lead miners, the 'soughs'. The aim of driving a sough was to drain water into a neighbouring valley that lies lower than the bottom of the mine, thus lowering the water table. Sometimes this meant tunnelling for miles, which could take decades. Usually the digging started near to the stream or river where the mine water was to drain. Several veins could be drained along one sough, so the immense investment of toil, time and (sometimes) lives appeared to be worth it to those who profited from the enterprise.

Soughs were being driven from early in the seventeenth century. A Dutch drainage expert, Sir Cornelius Vermuyden, was a favourite of Charles I because he was responsible for devising ways to drain the fens in Lincolnshire, thereby reclaiming immensely valuable and fertile agricultural land. He then came to the Derbyshire Dales to develop drainage for the Dove Gang mine between Cromford and Wirksworth. This, the 'Vermuyden Sough', is the first recorded and it took twenty years to complete. It was finished in 1631. Many others were to follow. Over 450 soughs were driven in the seventeenth, eighteenth and nineteenth centuries.

An area that attracted a great deal of interest and later investment was the Alport mining field. Since the mid seventeenth century, a number of soughs had been driven to drain the many veins running through Alport. But so valuable was Alport's lead, that the longest of all the soughs in Derbyshire, the Hillcarr Sough, was surveyed and constructed specifically to drain the Alport mines at a deeper level. Finance was raised by mine owners, smelters and by other shareholders. The long soughs were financed on the whole by venture capitalists that could make a profit from their share of the lead made available by the unwatering of the mines.

Hillcarr Sough

Work started in 1766 on driving Hillcarr Sough on the west bank of the River Derwent in Hillcarr Woods at Darley Dale. The tunnel was driven beneath Stanton Moor. A shaft was sunk to the level of the sough and then horizontal tunnels were excavated through the hillside to meet the shaft, then at each stage a further shaft was sunk. The immense undertaking was beset with difficulties. There were problems with ventilation and with the hardness of the rock and so progress was very slow. Boats were used to remove rock debris from the tunnel. It took twenty-one years before the Guy Vein at Alport was reached and the venture, at this stage, had cost £20,000. This became the longest sough in Derbyshire, at four and a half miles with its many branches running off it.

The work of driving the soughs was both difficult and dangerous. In 1774 a gas explosion injured several men. In 1777 six men '*were suffocated by the damp in ye driving of "Hill Carr Sough"*. Two of them, Thomas Willis and Richard Oldfield, were young men from Youlgrave. The other local men killed were from Stanton Lees, Stanton and Birchover. [11]

The River Bradford was itself a casualty of Hillcarr Sough. In 1882 something very dramatic occurred when the River Bradford disappeared down a mineshaft and (as proved by the fate of an unfortunate dog) flowed straight down Hillcarr Sough. Miss Fanny Thornhill Needham related the story to members of Youlgrave Women's Institute in 1931. A man came to tell her, ' "You'll never see Alport no more, it's all falling in!" *A milk cart had gone down a hole into an old shaft by the big tor (Raenstor) in Bradford. The hole was about as big as a house and hundreds of people came to see the strange sight of the river pouring down it – from Sheffield, Nottingham and Manchester. Loads of stones were carted to try and fill up the hole but it seemed to be no use at all. One day a man came over the hills from Baslow with a black retriever, to see how the hole was getting on. He foolishly threw a stick into the water for his dog which was unable to get out as the current was so strong. The man shouted he would give £5 to any man who would save it, but none would venture. Three weeks later the remains appeared in Darley.'*

Eventually the hole was sealed with brushwood but hydrologists believe that the disappearance of the River Bradford in times of drought can still be blamed on this giant drain. The daily flow from the tail of Hillcarr Sough has been recorded at between five and eight million gallons a day.

'They got all these riches from the minerals and now we're paying dearly because when they finished mining minerals, they didn't block it up, they didn't close the door, they left everything wide open. So all the soughs they've done, all the shattering of rock, it's all left open. Nobody had any money or the time left to put it right.'

Warren Slaney, Head River Keeper for Haddon Estate.

Fine stone arches support Hillcarr Sough 1980 (photo by Dickie Bird)

Cathedrals, castles, bridges, houses and churches: the great surviving edifices of past ages are a record of the craftsmanship, ingenuity and aesthetics of past engineers, builders and designers. The beauty and value of their work speaks to us of other times and has the power to move and inspire us today.

The skills used to great effect by the lead miners and sough drivers of Derbyshire are unseen by most of us, but now inspire awe and amazement among present day cavers, pot-holers and mining enthusiasts. A world exists below the ground, which is beyond the power of our imagination to envisage. A whole landscape of tunnels, chambers, shafts, machine housings and waterways lies within the limestone of the Derbyshire Dales. Tunnels lie under hillsides, criss-crossing under fields, and even under rivers in an underground world built by the lead miners and sough drivers. They have altered forever the hydrology of the White Peak. These amazing feats of structural engineering, underground navigation and unimaginable toil over many years have largely stood the test of time. But where soughs have collapsed or blocked, the impact on the rivers and land above ground is dramatic. Any consideration of the future of local water supplies in the area or of the health of its rivers in times of drought and flood must first consult the underground map of mines and soughs in the Dales.

Above : A leak in the Bradford riverbed

Left : Map of the mines, veins and soughs of Alport mining field (reproduced with permission from J. Rieuwerts)

Mist rising from the New Dam at Hollow Farm

Water Power

The mineral riches of Alport were such that the investment of driving the Hillcarr Sough was quickly repaid; in just two years profits were recorded. The next ambition of the mine owners was to extract from below the level of the sough, so they went ever deeper and encountered huge volumes of water. In the early days of the nineteenth century, the top engineering brains of the day were put to the task of unwatering the lead mines of Alport. Seven hydraulic engines, mostly powered by the Rivers Bradford and Lathkill, were installed underground. The great Cornish mining engineer and inventor Richard Trevithick devised the first of these engines in 1803, just two years after he had created the world's first steam locomotive in 1801.[12]

Trevithick's hydraulic engine was installed in the revealingly titled Crashpurse Mine (close to Hollow Farm) in 1805 and was considered to be an innovation of the greatest advance.

[12] Michael Mosley, scientist and broadcaster, has recently described Trevithick's high-pressure steam engine as 'the most extraordinary invention of all time. It made the Industrial Revolution possible; it made the modern world possible… he liberated power, and in doing so transformed the world.'

John Farey, the eminent geologist, mathematician and writer, wrote in 1810 to The Philosophical Magazine of the efficacy of the new hydraulic pumps:

'(Trevithick's engine) … has ever since effectually pumped that mine forty-eight feet below the sough, and enabled large profits to be obtained by the owners, instead of the ruin that had previously attended the concern, as the name implies. And further, that the steady and effectual operation of this machine, after six years' experience, has occasioned another to be lately erected in Bacon-close mine, near the same place.'

The Philosophical Magazine Jan – May 1811

The need for capital investment on a big scale led the three main companies working in the Alport mine fields (Hillcarr Sough, Shining Sough and Blythe Mines) to consolidate in 1839 to form the Alport Mining Company with John Taylor in charge. The mine workings were by now 140 feet below Hillcarr Sough.

A series of engines were put to work between 1805 and 1848 in different shafts, with varying degrees of success. A number of Trevithick's engines were installed at Alport and what is now Hollow Farm was once the home and centre of operations for his engineer, Page. One of Trevithick's engines was later moved to the Wills Founder Mine at Winster. Tons of machinery were lifted from hundreds of feet underground using just horsepower. Later this engine was recovered and installed as a major exhibit at the Peak District Mining Museum – a feat accomplished by members of the Peak District Historical Mines Society in the 1970s. The engines employed at Alport were the most technically advanced in use anywhere at the time. The largest of these, the Guy Engine, was installed in 1842, 210 feet below the surface. The waterpower needed to drive this engine was supplied from the River Lathkill. A wooden viaduct that supported iron pipes went right over Alport, close to the footbridge, feeding water from the River Lathkill into a tunnel in the hillside and thence to the mineshafts. The river water used to power the pumps, together with the pumped mine water, was discharged into Hillcarr Sough.

Ever more outlandish schemes were doomed to failure, because this area, so rich in mineral veins, was also the junction of deep underground waterways. Alport lies on the northern flank of the Stanton Syncline (a concave formation of the limestone) where water gathers. The mines were either overwhelmed with volumes of water during times of flood or, in dry periods, the river flows were insufficient to power the pumps to unwater the mines.

Lead mining was the most significant employer of men in Youlgrave from the eighteenth century through to the latter part of the nineteenth century, but by then there was a shift away from mining to quarrying. A number still worked both as farmers or farm labourers and lead miners, in dual occupation. Some of the miners travelled to work outside of Youlgrave. About forty men were employed at the Mandale Mine in Lathkill Dale in 1820 and others travelled to Sheldon.

By the 1850s the market for lead was declining and the Alport Mining Company folded, its equipment being sold at auction. The getting of rocks and minerals out of the ground had been essential to the livelihoods of people living along the River Bradford over generations. But the price of lead and the cost of getting it, both in financial terms and human lives lost, brought the industry to a final standstill in the 1930s.

Left : Peregrine photographed in a quarry near Buxton
Right : Shining Bank Quarry near Alport,
now a nature reserve

From Lead Mining to Quarrying

A change in the pattern of employment in Youlgrave becomes evident when comparing census records from the mid nineteenth century. In 1851, 181 men are recorded as lead miners in Youlgrave, and there were 2,265 lead miners in Derbyshire as a whole. In this same year, just one man in Youlgrave is recorded as a quarry worker, and there were only 312 in the whole of Derbyshire. Ten years later, the 1861 census records 1,057 quarry workers in Derbyshire. From 1871 there was a rapid decline in the number of lead miners. There were 103 in Youlgrave in 1871 but only 25 in 1891. This decline is matched by an exponential rise in the number of quarry workers. By 1871 there were 45. In the 1901 census just 248 lead miners are recorded in the whole of Derbyshire, but 2,488 were working in quarries.

The switch to quarrying in the nineteenth century took different forms. The value of gritstone for millstones and as a building material had been exploited for hundreds of years, and it continued to be used heavily. The close proximity of gritstone quarries on Stanton Moor, and all along the Derwent Valley, provided work for those that were prepared to travel a short distance.

Shining Bank Quarry (belonging to Haddon Estate), close to Alport, has ceased extracting limestone and is now on the way to becoming a nature reserve, but elsewhere large-scale stone quarrying continues.

The scars left on the Peak District landscape are reminders that even though this was Britain's first National Park (with many protection orders and planning restrictions), blasting, cutting and taking out of bedrock was and is 'business as usual'.

Minerals and Stone

Through the nineteenth century the minerals that were formerly discarded in the lead mining process ('gangue' materials) were gradually exploited, first in small-scale local industries, then later in much larger industrialised processes, many of which continue today. The valuable minerals extracted from within the limestone bedrock became the region's new mineral bonanza of the twentieth century. High up on the limestone plateau above and away from the River Bradford and its villages runs the Long Rake – one of the longest of all the mineral rakes of Derbyshire. It cuts across the high ground of what was once the commons of Middleton and Youlgrave Moors. On this plateau there are places of ancient pilgrimage, worship and burial: Bee Low and the great Neolithic henge of Arbor Low. They now lie alongside clanking, rumbling machinery as the work of breaking, crushing and washing rocks goes on at the site of two former mineral mines. Extraction of calcite, barytes and lead ore from the Long Rake came to an end when Middleton Mine (a site now occupied by Derbyshire Aggregates) closed in the 1970s, followed by the Long Rake Spar Company, which ceased production in 1981. This closed an era of mining that had spanned many hundreds of years. Derbyshire Aggregates and the Long Rake Spar Company now process stone brought in from quarries around Britain and other parts of the world. You can now build a henge in your garden with stone monoliths cut 'fit for purpose' from these stone processing companies. These days, on the Long Rake, the sounds of machinery, engines and air brakes from haulage trucks mingle with the song of larks; and hares dodge lorry wheels along the lane where, four thousand years ago, pilgrims once journeyed to worship their gods at Arbor Low.

Left : Long Rake Calcite Mine 1985 (photo by Dickie Bird)
Right : Youlgrave with the spoil heap from the doomed Mawstone Mine in the foreground

Mawstone Mine Disaster

An attempt to revive the fortunes of the lead mining industry in Youlgrave in the 1930s ended in tragedy. Mawstone Mine, which lies half a mile south of Youlgrave, had proved to be a troublesome mine and failed to prosper in the last decades of lead mining. Two companies that worked Mawstone Mine had gone under, the first in the 1880s and the second in the 1920s. But a persistent local belief in the possibility of great riches to be made from veins lying south-west of the mine led to the dangerous hunt for lead through shale. The gas given off by shale (principally methane, often referred to as 'firedamp') is highly flammable and very toxic, but despite this, the Mawstone Mine Company was intent on driving a new exploratory level through shale towards Gratton Dale. It was during an attempt at improving ventilation of this level that a fatal spark from a fan switch ignited gases that caused an explosion at 5.30pm on 23 May 1932.

Six men were down the mine at the time of the explosion: William Brindley, John Gallagher, Geoffrey Gould, Poultney Porter, James Porter and George Frost. George Frost, who was the only man to come out of the mine alive, just managed to get to the cage at the shaft bottom and signal to come up. The Mine Manager, Kenneth Seville, went straight down the mine and was overcome by fumes. He later returned to the mine with rescue parties of miners and other villagers. They went down armed only with handkerchiefs or caps held over their faces. Kenneth Seville headed one of the parties and two of the youngest Mawstone miners, Eric Evans and Jack Birds, ran from Youlgrave to join in the rescue attempt. All three of these men perished. Later at 7pm a mines rescue team from Chesterfield and Clay Cross came with breathing apparatus, but by then it was too late. Carbon monoxide poisoning had caused the death of all eight men.

The selfless rescue attempt by local men was described in the Derbyshire Times as *'Heroism unsurpassed in the history of mining.'* [13]

Father and son Poultney and James Porter were buried in their native Cumberland, while the funeral for Jack Birds took place at Youlgrave on Thursday 26 May. The funeral of the other five miners at Youlgrave church was held on Friday 27 May. The account of this in the Sheffield Independent conveys something of the terrible impact of this tragedy on the community of Youlgrave:

'Youlgrave mourned her lost sons yesterday. Five of the victims of the lead mine disaster were buried in the graveyard in the shadow of the ancient grey stone church upon the hill in sight of the mine in which they lost their lives … It was not until yesterday that the visitor could assess the severity of the blow the disaster has dealt to the little community of Youlgreave … But yesterday the whole village went into mourning, and the skies, so it seemed, wept in sympathy. The normal life of the village ceased. All the shops were shut, the mines and quarries in the immediate neighbourhood closed down, while in the village window blinds and curtains were drawn. Hundreds joined in the funeral procession, which must have been nearly the length

of the whole village street, and the majority of the mourners were of course, relatives of the men. Almost everybody in the village felt a personal grief, for not only were the victims known to all, but the majority of the inhabitants of Youlgreave were related to one or other of them.'

The end of lead mining in the White Peak came soon after the Mawstone Mine disaster, when the great Mill Close Mine at Darley Dale was closed in 1940.

John and Margaret Folley are brother and sister who have lived in Youlgrave all of John's life and for most of Margaret's. John has spent all his working life employed by Haddon Estate, working both on the land and in the house. Their father was a lead miner from Cumbria, who had worked in gold mines in South Africa before fighting in the trenches in the First World War. He came to Youlgrave in the 1920s to work first in the ill-fated Mawstone Mine and later at Mill Close Mine:

'If you get shale on a bed of limestone, under a bed of sandstone, you get gas. They went through the shale that made the firedamp and that's what caused the explosion.' [14]

Margaret remembers her father saying: ' *"If you go through the shale I'm leaving". So he left and went to work at Mill Close Mine. I can remember my father coming home at night. Sometimes he used to go on night shifts. He went over Stanton Moor. He used to come home wet through, because they used to work waist high in water to get the lead out. He was there when they closed the mine. We've got a lock and key that was in Mill Close Mine. My father grabbed the lock and key when they saw the water coming up and the manager said he could keep it (as a memento of the mine). It was the richest lead mine there was.*

He didn't talk about his work very often. The only thing he told us was "never walk in the woods when the (ground) covers up because there's that many open mine shafts you wouldn't know where they were."'

---

[13] A detailed account of the tragedy and its aftermath *The Mawstone Mine Disaster* by Andrew Mc Cloy and Norman Wilson was produced in 2007 as a tribute to those who died and others who tried to save them.
[14] The firedamp that Margaret describes is the name given to harmful gases that are produced by mining operations (especially coal mining). *Damp* derives from *dampf* (German for *vapour*).

This admonition didn't stop John from exploring and enjoying the peculiar fascination of deep dark holes in the ground.

'Up on Youlgrave Moor there's a shaft at Long Rake, between where Back Lane meets Moor Lane. It's 450 feet deep and it was open at this time. There was barbed wire around it, but I used to climb over it and have a look down the shaft. If you threw a stone down you could hear it bounce against the side boom, boom, boom. What you could hear a long way down was the rush of water. If the top of Long Rake's 1,000 feet and Youlgrave's only 600 feet. It would come 50 feet down this road to Alport. They've covered it up now.'

Mill Close Mine had been one of the most productive lead mines in the world and its final closure after overwhelming floods spelt the end of many hundreds of years of lead mining in the Peak District.

'It flooded in 1939 and it was like the Titanic going down, when one level filled up, then another level filled up and then another and they had to come out of it. That was in 1939 when it finished.'

Mawstone Mine in the 1930s (photo provided by Andrew McCloy from *The Bugle*)

Part 4

Restoring the River: the River Keeper's Project

'The Bradford was always the richest river … a nice mix of limestone gorge and gritstone catchment … It's a really useful nursery stream for everything. The bigger rivers don't produce very many small fish … The Wye is good, the Lathkill is superb, but the Bradford is the best.'

Warren Slaney, Head River Keeper for Haddon Estate

Weir at Brookleton

Each of the six dams of Middleton and Bradford Dale has its own character and atmosphere. This relates not only to their actual location in the dale, but also to the various uses made of them in the past. The dams in the lower part of the river were built specifically for use as fish pools for Haddon Estate's trout fishing. The white gate across the river path towards Middleton used to separate land owned by the Waterhouses of Middleton Hall and that owned by Haddon Estate, but now Haddon owns and manages all of the River Bradford from the top of the dale to the confluence at Alport.

The fishery used to work by stocking brown trout that were hatched near Conksbury. This kind of river keeping is unnatural, but has dominated the fly-fishing industry for many years. Today the river is home to wild brown trout, and the management of the river is aimed at restoring the natural balance of the river and all of its ecosystems.

Warren Slaney, who is Head River Keeper for the Haddon Estate, has the management of stretches of the Derwent, the Wye and the Lathkill, and all of the Rivers Bradford and Daykin. His project and long-term goal for the River Bradford has been to unravel the river from its past. Since the first Corn Mill Dam was made in the distant past, the flow of the river has been slowed in places and accelerated in others. It has been widened, diverted, and generally modified. But it was the Victorians who had the greatest impact on the appearance and flow of the river, creating dams

for the mills and for trout. The sluice gates on each of the six dams have boards that can be raised or lowered to control water levels and flows in an intensively managed system. Warren explains:

'We lift the dams to allow fish to migrate and to move silt. If it isn't moved it builds up and if anything happens and the dam is let go in one go (sabotage, or sluice or dam failure) the river will be stone dead. We refit it wearing dry suits and seal the leaks so it remains full for as much of the summer as possible.'

Above : Comfrey growing on the banks of the Corn Mill Dam

Left : The screw mechanism in the fourth dam releases water by raising a board fitted in the dam wall

Above : Boathouse Dam full in spring
Left : Outflow over the weir on the fourth dam

Above : Moorhen
Left : Warren Slaney (photo by Adam Gray)
Right : Marsh marigolds in May on the third dam

Many people have come to associate Bradford Dale with its expanses of still water and, by contrast, the rushing weirs. But the appearance and behaviour of the river is changing and it isn't just because of the weather. Warren has been taking the river back in time, to allow it to flow as it might have done 300 years ago. In this part of the book he outlines his project as he described it to the author in several walks along the river.

Along Bradford Dale the valley floor is twenty-five and thirty metres higher at the opening of the main gorge below Middleton Dale than it is at the end, at Holywell. This considerable drop in level would once have channelled a narrow but fast-flowing stream driven just by gravity or 'head loss'. The six dams along the dale now account for around half this drop and have taken the energy from the river by halting its natural flow. Warren explains:

'A river operates far better when it has a continuous flow of water, transmitting velocity (flow) from head loss, rather than through vertical falls. This allows water crowfoot (Ranunculus flutitans) to grow, which holds back the water in times of low flow, and creates pockets for animals and fish to live in. It also pinches the flow to cause fast runs of water, which are important for inject-breathing trout and flow-dependent insects. Previously it was thought that water needed to be constantly dropped in order to be charged with oxygen. We now know this is not the case. Water in a river is almost always 100% saturated in oxygen (the levels fluctuate through pressure and temperature) and does not need to be dropped from weirs to oxygenate itself.'

A Natural Flow

'We changed the system away from stocking fish when the river was treated like one great big fish farm. It didn't matter whether the fish survived over winter, they could all disappear because the fish lorry came next year and we stocked again. This is no good for things in the wild because nothing had anything to eat over the winter.

We tried to envisage how wide the Bradford would be if you take out the boards and then narrow it to its natural width. You have to come up to the Bradford to see where it forms a channel through the watercress to understand the river. So we came up here and watched these reed beds and then took that measurement down to the Coach Road and then formally made it that width all the way down through the Coach Road. The water is so wide across the dam and yet its natural width is only two metres.

It's saying "I don't want all this, this is not necessary for me because this is all the flow I've got and this is all the flow that the Ranunculus needs, and the fish need, and the insects need, so all the rest you can have".

A natural meander would take place all along the river as it cuts into the bank and worms back on itself. This is how it wants to be. It doesn't want to be in a straight line. I would love these dams to be taken out one day and the river put back in its natural course again. Over time, these dams are just going to disappear into a soggy silty bog. There would never be an impervious, impenetrable dam on a natural river. It would go round it, through or under it.'

'The River Bradford had been over-widened. What Warren has managed to do, is encourage the equilibrium to go back to reflect the flow regime and by allowing the channel to narrow down has made it a much more natural system. It has created a regime of pools and riffles that reflect much more what a natural river would look like.'

Fred Baker, Ecological Consultant

Top left : The river finding its own way through the riparian weeds
Left : Third dam with very little weed in 2006   **Right** : Same view photographed in 2012

'Over time, left entirely alone, all this greenery will become land and you'll be able to walk on it. It will be marshy in the winter time when it floods but it will slowly form a flood plain and the river will etch and bend and meander nicely through this flood plain all the time, for the rest of humanity and beyond.'

Spawning Beds

'This is our spawning bed. This is the most important piece of the river, and when we've got herons in the trees, we know that it's spawning time because they know the trout are spawning here.

We drive a little mini-tractor in here and we dig all this gravel up when the fish arrive in mid-winter so they can spawn on some clean gravel around the shortest day. We have to break it all up so the fish can work it with their tails and lay their eggs in the gravel.

Roller Brook isn't fenced, so the cattle can stand in the stream and all the suspended solids, all the soil, comes down the dams and settles out between the gravels here and clogs it up. We'll get in here in November, six or seven of us, with picks and shovels and we'll make sure it's shining again. Every time you turn a stone underneath it's clean, the top is covered in algae, so you turn it with a shovel and pick and it becomes clean.

In a natural river there would be new amounts of gravel coming into the river all the time. Gravel works its way down but it's always entering at the top and that works through a natural system where the river erodes, cuts gravel out of the soil and then gets it into the channel and rolls it down. Rain scours into the bank (dale-side) and it undercuts and you have a collapse of scree. The fish would be on it straight away and it all grades nicely, bigger bits earlier and the fine stuff further down.'

Warren would like to see fencing to stop cattle from going in the river along much of the length of the Bradford. As it is, he has to keep on cleaning the gravel. But it is not only the trout that would benefit from protecting the margins of the stream. The banks and waterside plants are home to water vole, refuge for water fowl and rich with insects.

Left : Spawning area in third dam

'If you let cattle in, they eat all the mineral-rich semi-emergent plants and the river will be over-wide and then we've got algae. We used to come up here and cut out the weed, but that can be destructive as it's full of insects. A lot of rivers have lost their insects and there is a coordinated national river-fly monitoring scheme which we take part in. There are plenty of insects here though.

This is a nursery. There are baby fish here – they're like ghosts, they disappear and then they're in view again. They grow in the margins of the weed, safe from the adult fish and they grow and slowly take up territory as they drift down the river, all the way down.

The trout is an inject breather. Here the water is going in through its mouth and out through its gills because of the flow. If you take the flow off, it needs to find the flow through its mouth and gills like a lake trout would, by swimming around. This fish is healthy because of the way the river is operating. If there aren't the insects here it will lose condition and have to drop out and find some other territory.'

Top left : Nettles, meadowsweet, watercress, hairy willowherb and other riparian plants dominate the riverside in summer
Below : Baby brown trout find refuge in the weed

Top : Brown trout **Middle** : Heifer paddling at Brookleton with heron and mallards
Bottom : Dipper in the shallows

Cutting the Redd

'The trout's nest is called a redd. She cuts a nest with her tail and lays the eggs. Quite often there is a precocious male who tries to dash in just as she's laying her eggs. You've got a big male waiting because he's fought off all the other contenders and he's ready to mate with her and a little precocious male will try to nip in and mate with her quickly. The dominant male's job is to fight everything off until that last possible second. Then it's done and those two fish have spawned properly in the right place.

I think that our brown trout are looking for up-swelling seams of water to lay their eggs in. If it's true, it's pretty incredible that they know that their eggs will survive better in springs that come through the riverbed.

This is one of the things I enjoy about not stocking. Only the absolute fittest can survive. These are the ones that jump the weirs, get to the spawning bed, get to it at the right time, are able to avoid the herons and fight off the other males and, if they are the females, the ones able to 'cut the redd' exactly right.'

'All along the dale, I'd like just sheep. The river's so important that it actually dictates how the land around it is used – then you can start to dictate what stock goes on. I'd like to see summer hay, winter sheep, never any cattle, never any herbicides. That's what we do on the Lathkill below Raper. The Bradford isn't seen to be that important at the moment.

When baby fish hatch out, this is perfect for them. They'll drift down, they'll find new territories and habitats further down and restock the river where their parents came from. We've got control of the whole of the Bradford. Nobody can stock it with any other fish and bring disease in there, and we can look after the top reaches and that controls our destiny. All my predecessors were sceptical. One of them said, "if you're not stocking (trout) again, or out of a job, I'll eat my hat". Financially it's a radical move and a financial risk, but we've proved it works, and we've managed to get other people to do it.'

'This section of the river just produces insects for the dippers and wagtails. The shallow braided flow here doesn't have the depth to support fish. There are ten different rivulets across it. Once upon a time this would have been a clear riffle where the fish used to spawn, but the cattle have pushed soil out into the river, so it's become over-wide. I believe there used to be a wall along here. You need diversity in a river. You need deep water for adult fish and shallow water for the little ones, and other water for insects. It's good for everything here, apart from fish.'

Native white-clawed crayfish (photo by Karen Shelley-Jones, PDNPA)

White-clawed Crayfish (*Austropotamobius pallipes*)

The white-clawed crayfish is the UK's only native crayfish and its largest freshwater invertebrate. They were once widespread and could be found in both still and running water. They are particularly associated with clean, hard-water streams and rivers, favouring habitats that have overhanging bank-side vegetation, roots, submerged rotting logs, and stones or boulders. These features combine to provide white-clawed crayfish with shelter, food and cover.

The River Bradford is now one of the only rivers in the Peak District to have a population of the native crayfish. They were once common and widespread but they are now rare, as their numbers have been devastated by the introduction of the North American signal crayfish. This species was introduced to the UK in the 1970s for the seafood trade and is now present in large numbers in the wild. It is larger than the native crayfish, more aggressive and breeds faster. Critically, the signal crayfish has brought with it a virulent plague that has wiped out the natives in many parts of England. The plague can also be spread by water, fishing equipment or boots that have been in contaminated water. Other animals may also spread the spores of the plague.

The white-clawed crayfish is now a species of global conservation concern and is classified as Endangered by the International Union for the Conservation of Nature (IUCN). Its continued presence in the River Bradford tells us a lot about the quality of habitat and about the diligent and sensitive management of the river.

The conservation of this population of native crayfish in the River Bradford will depend on three things: maintaining suitable habitat conditions, including water quantity and quality; protecting individuals that remain; and, crucially, preventing the spread of signal crayfish and crayfish plague into the river.

River flies in high summer

'The Bradford's part of a group now: The Peacock Fly Fishing Club, a local club that has got fishing on the Wye, the Lathkill and the Bradford. They have had chapter and verse about biosecurity. They make sure all their nets are cleaned off and they don't wade, they don't step in the water so they don't take any alien invertebrates from elsewhere'

It isn't only the weather or disease and predation from alien species that threaten the river and its creatures. The catchment for the River Bradford covers an immense acreage of over forty farms. The flow of a river may be affected by water taken from the ground (through abstraction) and its water quality by substances put or spilled on the land.

'A lorry could tip over on the A6 on the Wye or we could have an acute pollution from a farmer that doesn't understand. The old type of organo-phosphate sheep dip was much more harmful to people but less harmful to insects in the river. The modern synthetic pyrethroid sheep dips are a hundred times more poisonous to river flies. On the River Dove, a while ago they lost all their river flies through Beresford Dale. All the dippers (thirteen of them) had gathered together in a single pool, and that was the first indication that something was wrong. They went upstream and found that all the insects were dead. None of the fish were dead. Gradually over time, everything moved on and the river became completely dead. The sheep dip can get into the river from the sheep or be irresponsibly dumped.

The Bradford was killed some time in the late 1970s when a slurry tank burst at Elton. All of the rivers are always on the brink between happiness and existence and an awful acute pollution that we could suffer any day.'

The Perfect Moment

'After the mayfly around the end of June if the air pressure is right and you are on the Bradford in the evening there are kilos of blue-winged olive spinners that are returning to the river to lay their eggs. This happens two or three times a week an hour before dusk. A column that stretches across both banks to the top of the trees all the way from Alport to the top of Middleton Dale is full of returning male insects all hatched from the river and ready to return to the river to mate with the females. These are the columns of dancing males, the females fly underneath, copulate and fall away to die, which is when the fish come and take them. The fish feed from the flies as nymphs, when they've hatched and when they return to die. If the day is right for the flies to hatch, then it is likely it's right for them to lay their eggs and then die so that the insects' bodies aren't lost to the fish through inclement weather. The river flies don't have mouthparts so they don't have to feed, so it's just that one perfect moment when they hatch, mate and die. The blue-winged olive represents ninety-eight per cent of insects on the river.'

Like the mayfly, the blue-winged olive spinners are 'ephemera' – for the day.

Blue-winged olive spinners lie dead on the river

Young heron with brown trout

'The Bradford was always the richest river. It's richer than the Lathkill, which is a harsh environment - its pH is very high. The Bradford is a nice mix of limestone gorge and gritstone catchment, and it's a got a good pH. That's why you've got the weed and the crustaceans. Gammarus, the water shrimp, likes it because it builds its exoskeleton from the calcium. They're able to shed their skeletons quicker so they grow quicker. There were always more crayfish here than in the Lathkill.

All the keepers think the Bradford's a better river than the Lathkill. If I didn't have the River Bradford, I'd really want it, to manage it correctly. It's a really useful nursery stream for everything, for the Lathkill, the Wye and the Derwent. The bigger rivers don't produce very many small fish, but the Wye is good, the Lathkill is superb, but the Bradford is the best.'

Part 5

The Future

'It will rise, in a time after times …
It will return stainless
For the delivery of this world.'

Ted Hughes, *The River*, 1983

Dawn over Stanton Moor and Bradford Dale

Snowdrifts above Youlgrave December 2010

The Little Ice Age

'Memoriall of the great snow.

This year, 1614-15, January 16, began the greatest snow which ever fell upon the earth, within man's memorye. It covered the earth five quarters deep uppon the plain. And for heap or drifts of snow, they were very deep; so that passengers both horse and foot, passed over gates, hedges and walls. It fell at ten several times and the last was the greatest, to the great admiration and fear of all the land for it came from the four points of the world, so that all entries were full yey the south parte as well as these mountains. It continued by daily increasing until the twelfth day of March (without the sight of any earth either upon hills or valleys) Uppon which day (being the Lord's day) it began to decrease: and so by little and little consumed and wasted away until the eight and twentieth day of May for then all the heaps or drifts of snow were consumed except one upon Kinder's Scout which lay til Whitson Week and after Hindrances and losses in this peak country by the snow above sayed one.'

The 'swimming pool', Brookleton August 2011 (photo by Andrew McCloy)

'1615, A Dry Summer
there was no rain fell upon the earth'
Entry in Youlgrave Parish Records

Europe and North America experienced an extended period of bitterly cold winters, often referred to as the 'Little Ice Age', between 1550 and 1850[1]. Climate scientists have considered the various natural causes for this, including decreased sunspot activity, volcanic eruptions and altered ocean circulation. A drought followed on from this perishing winter in a pattern that was repeated in 2011. Four hundred years ago a Youlgrave church warden recorded this extreme weather event for posterity. Then, as now, our obsession with the weather reflects our underlying knowledge that ultimately our survival depends on what it does. While writing this, much of the Derbyshire Dales area lies under deep snow in late March.

[1] The period as defined by NASA.

Bradford Dale December 2010

Climate Change and Extreme Weather

The geological events that shaped the Derbyshire Dales were partly caused by the effects of climate change that occurred in a time frame of hundreds of thousands of years. We are now experiencing climate change caused by human activity that is happening at an unprecedented rate. We have delved into the earth and exposed, mined and drilled for the long-buried, fossilised remains of previous life forms: the fossil fuels – oil, coal and natural gas. By burning up these remnants of other life forms we have warmed the earth. We now live in a different world from the one we inhabited only fifty years ago. Carbon dioxide and other greenhouse gas emissions caused by human activity are higher than ever before, and now the concentration of atmospheric carbon dioxide is at its highest level in twenty million years. Global warming is causing massive ice melts,

which have released huge volumes of freshwater into our oceans, leading to rising sea levels. Flooding has caused devastation to those living in low-lying areas. Some people have lost their homes, their land, and even their lives, as sea levels have risen.

Weather systems are regulated by the oceans, and when the temperature and the composition of the oceans change as radically as they are doing now, the effects on our weather cannot be fully predicted. Based on evidence from past climate change cycles, the release of freshwater into the oceans could, ironically, make the UK much colder. For people living in marginal lands across the globe, desertification, crop failure and famine have been just some of the consequences. All of this appeared to be happening a long way from us until recently, when we experienced our own extreme weather events.

[2] Environment Agency data.

What's Happened to the River?

The River Bradford dried up entirely between 12 August and 8 December 2011. It was the dismay and deep-seated unease felt by residents of Youlgrave, Middleton and Alport, who saw their treasured river cease to flow, that gave rise to a packed public meeting in November 2011. The cracked and dried-out riverbed, the puddles from which gasping fish and crayfish were rescued by the bucket-load – these have been shocking reminders of how fragile our water supply is.

From October 2010 to September 2011 rainfall data for the catchment that includes the Bradford was the seventh-driest year on record. The summer of 2011 was the fourth-driest ever (1995–96 had been the driest year ever).[2]

People all over the drought-afflicted regions of Britain experienced water shortages, dried-up rivers and crop failure. In Youlgrave and the surrounding villages, the question from locals and visitors alike was 'What's happened to the river?'

Dried riverbed August 2011 (photo by Andrew McCloy)

Rain had not fallen, as weeks and months went by in the previous autumn, winter, then summer. The drought ended spectacularly with immense rainfall that recharged the river in December 2011. By contrast, 2012 was the year of floods, with the heaviest spring rains on record. Many people in Britain had their towns, businesses and homes flooded repeatedly. Analysis of weather patterns and river levels has shown that many rivers in Britain have gone from record low levels to highest-ever levels in a matter of months. Lord Chris Smith, the Environment Agency chairman, has said:

'It was an extraordinary year and it serves as a warning for the country that we face a future in which there are likely to be more and more extreme weather events. We need, very urgently, to prepare plans to deal with these extremes.'[3]

The impact on the local river system of high rainfall has been, at times, dramatic. Water gushed from the head cave of the River Lathkill, streams roared off the hillsides, and springs were recharged. Farmers struggled to mow their silage and hay. Cattle came in early, as the fields were too waterlogged for them to feed. Floods lay for weeks across the fields of the Derwent Valley. The water table was at its highest level for years. The River Bradford was restored and became full of energy and life. In the space of twelve months we had witnessed locally what has been occurring across the world – extreme weather. While it is not possible to make a clear causal link between specific weather events and climate change, scientists have stated that unpredictable and extreme weather is a consequence of our climate changing.

Far left : May 2006
Middle : August 2011 (photo by Andrew McCloy)
Left : Flooded fields at Bradford December 2012

[3] The Observer, 3 March 2013.

Drought and Flood

Like all rivers, the flow of the Bradford varies immensely according to rainfall. Rivers in limestone areas do disappear from time to time. Locals report many periods in the past when the river has ceased to flow during long dry spells in the summer, and most especially in the summers following winters with low rainfall.

The drought of 2011 left trout struggling and often dying in shallow puddles. Many were rescued and moved on to the Lathkill, but there were many losses. The rare and endangered white-clawed crayfish also had to be rescued and moved into secure areas. The drought had a major impact right through the river's food chain.

'The birds could move so I don't think they suffered in the drought. One of my under keepers comes every month of the year to check the insects in the river by taking kick-samples (samples are obtained by literally kicking at the river bed to disturb the invertebrates that live there). He says that right up until the end of July, in the last couple of weeks before we lost the river on the 12 August 2011, we had plenty of insects. They crashed. There was still enough water, just not enough oxygen, and they died in their billions.'

Warren Slaney

After a period of sustained rainfall in November and in early December 2011 the river began to flow once more.

'It rained twenty-two or twenty-four millimetres that night, and the river came back on 8 December. As the river was coming back we went up the Lathkill. It's interesting when the river comes back, you can see it recharging through the base. You've only got one chance in the year to catch it. You find out where the leaks are as well. It always seems to happen at night, so we came with head-torches and we could see the river coming back in. And in the little flow, you could see the nymphs – the mayfly nymphs coming from water that has been able to survive the drought up above. So at the very leading edge of water there were insects, and I think they do it to exploit the new environment. I've heard that the Gamarrus (water shrimp) come back the day after the water comes back. The water is teeming with Gamarrus. They can't fall from the sky, so where do they come from? The cavers have seen them underground but not in the numbers we see.'

The recovery of a river, while seeming miraculous, is not an instant process. The precarious ecosystems of the river require sensitive management.

'We rested the river for a year and made sure that nobody fished it. We wanted first of all to assess what was left and we wanted the fish to spread out naturally.'

Warren Slaney

Far top left : Summer downpour in Bradford Dale

Left : May downpour on the Coach Road

Above : Flow from the head cave in Lathkill Dale January 2013

Right : September 2012

Youlgrave Waterworks

Youlgrave Waterworks has maintained a proud tradition of self-sufficiency in the village water supply and has kept the taps flowing since 1829. Villagers are shareholders in this limited company and a long-standing committee made up of volunteers has had the hard task of managing the supply, infrastructure, maintenance and finances. Youlgrave Waterworks Ltd is almost unique in being one of the last independent (and British-owned) water companies, and is probably the oldest in the country.

Youlgrave and Bradford Dale from the east

Members of the Youlgrave Waterworks Committee outline the challenges and achievements of supplying water to the community from the surrounding landscape:

'If any institution can be said to be environmentally friendly, then Youlgrave Waterworks certainly is. It is a non-profit-making organisation run by board members, most of whom give their time voluntarily, and has been thus since 1829. Water from Bleakley Spring is collected using a recently installed balancing tank at the side of the spring in Bleakley Wood and piped to the village. The water travels to the village entirely by gravity, using only a small amount of electricity on the way at a small treatment plant at the side of Mawstone Lane, which is used to trickle-charge twenty-four-volt batteries to supply the treatment injectors.

The only other electrical use is at the Pinfold Pumping Station near the top of the village, where a small pump intermittently starts up to pressurise the system at the highest part of the village – a total power consumption of around three kilowatts.

This is the situation when there is adequate flow from the spring in times of plentiful rainfall, as was the case in 2012. If the spring output falls during dry weather, we have to supplement the spring with water from Mawstone Mine. In this case the level of Bleakley tank is monitored, and, should the level fall below a preset point, one of the submersible pumps at Mawstone starts up and continues to run until the level in Bleakley tank is restored. The pumps have not been used at all throughout 2012 due to the record rainfall.

If the water from Bleakley Spring is not used by the village (as is the case overnight), it fills the tank and then overflows and runs down Bleakley Dike into the New Dam, and then down to the River Bradford, joining the river at the bottom of Bradford Road. If the water were not collected by the village and allowed to run freely to the river it would not affect the level of the water in Bradford Dale and Middleton Dale in any way whatsoever, as Bleakley Dike joins the river way below the point where there has been much speculation about river levels.

Any leaks we find, or are reported by members of the community, are repaired almost immediately. Nevertheless demand on the village water supply continues to increase. This may be due to several reasons: there are new houses, more tourism, holiday homes; and modern household appliances use a lot of water. Because of this, the constraints of an abstraction level set many years ago is becoming harder and harder to adhere to. The present level of twenty-two million gallons was set in 1978, some thirty-five years ago and was reduced then from a previously agreed limit of twenty-seven million gallons. We don't know why. We believe it was when the supply was taken from two springs, one of which, the Harthill Moor Spring, ceased to be viable and so Bleakley Spring became the primary source. Some big utilities (allegedly) lose more than this in leakage alone.'

Youlgrave Waterworks

The hills where springs rise that supply water to Youlgave viewed from Moor Lane

This is cattle and sheep country and what gets put on the land sometimes finds its way into the water supply; anything from farm effluent to fertiliser:

'When I was first on the waterworks it wasn't treated at all. One spring had nitrates in it because the farmers were spreading that much around. So we had to abandon that spring in the 1980s. Each spring was tested, as we had to look for other sources.'

Malcolm Stacey

'Bleakley Spring water comes off millstone grit and is totally different from the water in Bradford Dale, as it is very soft and slightly acidic. This is treated at the Mawstone Lane meter pit by the injection of a small amount of caustic soda solution (which is a strong alkaline). This, when added at the correct level, neutralises the acid in the water to arrive at pH7, which is the neutral point. This pH is checked daily at the Pinfold Pumping Station.'

Youlgrave Waterworks

The waterworks committee (many of whom have served for decades) have had the job of keeping the supply going from the tricky local underground water systems. Once again the lead mines and soughs are part of the story as now a reliable source of water comes from Mawstone Mine (water from the blocked Hillcarr Sough).

'A stroke of luck is Hillcarr Sough collapsing! Under this hillside now there is an absolute Carsington Reservoir. It doesn't matter how much we pump it (ten hours a day sometimes) it never changes.'

Malcolm Stacey

'Even when the river was dry, the water levels in Mawstone Mine remained constant. The collapse of the sough caused the water level in Mawstone Mine to rise some twelve metres and this level has been maintained ever since the collapse of Hillcarr Sough. This has been rather fortunate for Youlgrave Waterworks, because in 2010–2011, during a very dry year, it was a very valuable back-up as the output of the spring depleted during that period as you would expect. The depth of the water in the mine hardly varied at all. It would affect Youlgrave Waterworks dramatically if the present situation with the sough were to change in any way.'

Youlgrave Waterworks

'The moment there's a leak it's reported, it's either next day or the day after it's repaired, as we can't afford to have treated water going into the ground. We take a little bit of pride in that – we don't lose water.'

Malcolm Stacey

'Personally I think it's first class water. If I go on holiday and come back the first thing I do is have a drink of Youlgrave water. It's a godsend. The important thing is, we keep it going for the next generation and how we do that I'm not sure. We have never got enough money.'

Eric Goodwin

'I think it's worth it to the village from a historical point of view. We've had it since 1829. The quality of water is better than you'd get from a water authority and if we gave it up we'd be taken over by them and the water wouldn't be as good. We've got to keep it going for as long as we can.'

Gordon Coupe

Managing Change

Fred Baker is an ecologist and director of a nationwide environmental consultancy. He has lived in Youlgrave and Alport all his life and was a founder member of both Sustainable Youlgrave *(see Appendix 6)* and the Bradford River Action Group (BRAG). Much of his work is focussed on sustainable development and finding ways to mitigate the effects of human activity upon the environment.

'We have to make sure that water use and supply at both ends of the pipe are managed properly to allow us to cope with the extreme events we are likely to get. We have to look both at reducing use and making sure we've got sufficient supply during extreme events – particularly drought.

As a society we have to build greater resilience into what we do or we won't be able to adapt to climate change. A small country should be able to respond quickly to increase or loss of water. We must build in resilience to extended drought or we won't get through. Government understands it, and many communities understand but there is a gap between national policy and local implementation. We have the ability to adapt, we're a rich country and we're well organised but we've got to recognise that adaptation has to begin now. Everything that we do must be considered against the background of climate change. All the forward policy, the decision-making processes have to have that as background and national government has done that but it's got to filter right down through society. We need to get rid of policies that restrict adaptation to climate change. Our biggest challenge will be reducing energy used by our current housing stock. We have to change the fabric of our buildings. Our current approach to conservation doesn't achieve that. We need to farm more sustainably, without artificial fertilisers and we need 'closed loop' farming practice where the main energy input is from the sun.'

Fred Baker

Sun rising behind Harthill Castle Ring and Robin Hood's Stride

The Future for the River Bradford

So what might the future hold for the River Bradford? Dryer conditions in the dale's woodlands, adjacent fields, and nearby dewponds as well as loss of flow in the river would have an impact on invertebrates, amphibians, fish, mammals and birds. Reduced flows lead to a decline in water quality and to algal bloom. This in turn leads to fish deaths and lack of food for river birds such as the dipper, kingfisher, heron and grey wagtail. Riparian (between land and stream) plants may not survive, which would cause great damage to biodiversity throughout the river and its environs. Non-native species could flourish in the new conditions and alter the ecology.

While the strong flows that followed on from the drought were a cause for celebration in 2012, flooding can also cause great damage to a river's ecosystems. Floods in May 2008 washed away a colony of water voles that had established themselves on the River Bradford after a long period of absence. Both kingfishers and dippers lost their nests along the Lathkill, Derwent and Bradford in the floods of 2012. Spawning gravels can be washed away or covered in sediments. During periods with unusually high rainfall, manure and chemicals run off the land to pollute the rivers. Floods cause damage to riverbanks and sometimes wash important river weeds away.

'The structure of a river will adjust to a flow regime. If that flow regime is very variable, so we get more drought and more frequent flooding events, biodiversity will inevitably be reduced because the stability will have gone. Biodiversity responds to a certain level of perturbation. So the most biodiverse habitats are those that are disturbed on an intermediate level. Those systems that are completely stable have less biodiversity as there's no change, but equally systems that are subject to high levels of perturbation are less biodiverse because nothing can establish itself. Extended drought events could get rid of the invertebrate population for certain sections of the river or we may lose crayfish because the river dries out too frequently and there would be knock-on effects in terms of birds on the river (and fish). So we're likely to see the biodiversity drop with extremes in flow.'

Fred Baker

Above : Clapper bridge at Holywell

Top right : Water crowfoot (*Ranunculus flutitans*) helps the flow of the river and shelters waterfowl, insects, fish, amphibians, and water voles

Away from the river another major environmental impact on Bradford Dale could be the loss of many or all of the ash trees to the deadly Chalara Ash Dieback Disease. The impact on woodland throughout Britain is incalculable but especially so in the calcareous soils of the White Peak, where ash provides the dominant tree cover and is important both to the landscape and to biodiversity. *(See Appendix 5.)*

There are different ideas about how the river should flow and what made it stop flowing. The science of climate change is incontrovertible, but how we respond as a society, as a community and individually, to the challenges we face in future will depend on our ability to be fluid, like the river itself. The world that we have made has not been kind to our fellow creatures. But we can watch a dipper or grey wagtail working the river, follow a trout as it changes colour through light and shade, enjoy the dance of a million river flies or just gaze at the ever-changing surface of the stream. By doing these things we connect to the best part of what we are – living creatures being in the moment with other living things. We are all ephemera.

Self-portrait in a bubble

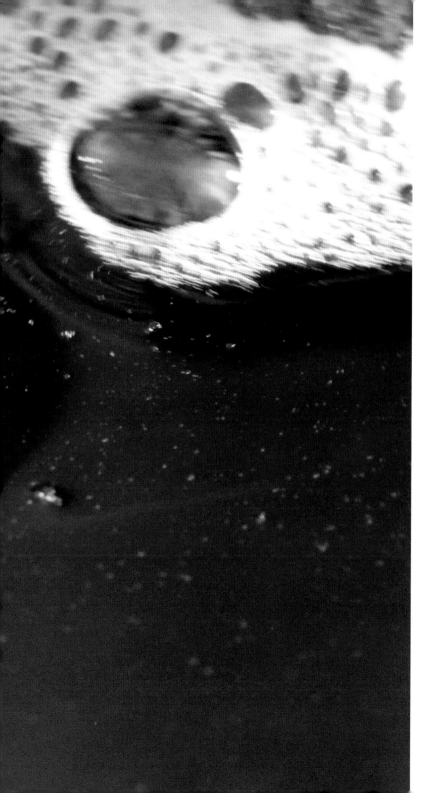

Spring reflection

Storm clouds to the south of Bradford Dale

Appendices

Appendix 1: Geology of the Peak District

The foundations of the landscape we see today in the Peak District were laid in the early part of what is called the Carboniferous Period. Our world was then unimaginably different from that which we inhabit now. The limestone of the White Peak was being formed around 360 to 310 million years ago when the part of the Earth's crust that is now Britain lay just south of the equator. Tectonic activity over millennia has shifted the Earth's surface and our part of it has been moving northwards, a process that is still going on.

The limestone in the Derbyshire Dales is composed of the fossilised remains of the shells and skeletons of creatures that lived in a warm, shallow tropical sea. As they died, the hard parts of these marine creatures (composed of calcium carbonate) sank to the seabed, to eventually form sediments. Over millions of years the sediments compressed into layers of what became limestone. This occurred at the rate of around one centimetre every hundred years.

While most of the remains of the creatures were crushed or fragmented by pressure and water action, certain whole fossils are evident in the Derbyshire limestone. The most common of these fossils are crinoids and brachiopods. Crinoids are sometimes called sea lilies but they are, in fact, animals that are related to today's starfish. Brachiopods were filter-feeding, bivalved shellfish.

Continuous movement of the Earth's crust had formed great mountains to the north at an earlier time. As these mountains were worn down by erosion, south-flowing rivers transported enormous quantities of sediments. During the Carboniferous period, the debris gradually encroached on this area and first clouded the tropical sea, then smothered it and eventually covered and buried the limestone that was formed from its creatures. This mass of sedimentary deposits, over millennia, resulted in the formation of an immense river delta, covering much of northern England. The mud and other fine materials settled out to form shales, and coarser materials produced the Millstone Grit of the Dark Peak.

Over millions of years, extreme pressure compressed and hardened the gravel, sand and mud of the delta into layers of gritstones, sandstones and shales that lay over the limestone. Compression and eventual fossilisation of the remains of trees and plants, from the forests which had covered much of the delta, created Coal Measures which now lie either side of the Peak District. However, many millions of years were still to pass before the formation of the Peak District as we recognise it today.

At the end of the Carboniferous period, around 290 million years ago, an intense period of tectonic activity resulted in immense pressure being exerted on the deep limestone rock strata, which now lay below two kilometres of younger rocks.

The limestone buckled under the pressure of earth movements, and faults, cracks and fissures formed in it. Under the weight and heat generated by the depth of the rocks, hot mineralised fluids rich in lead, zinc, barium and fluorine were squeezed into the limestone from the surrounding shales that had previously trapped and locked in these elements. The fluids cooled and solidified underground, leading to the formation of mineral crystals along veins within the fractured limestone mass. The exploitation of these valuable mineral deposits that are threaded through the limestone is central to the social and economic development of the Derbyshire Dales.

The Derbyshire Dome

Ever-continuing tectonic activity led to the formation of the Derbyshire Dome, which was the result of great horizontal force being exerted on the rocks and causing them to buckle and rise. This pressure, gradually over millennia, led to folding and faulting that can be seen in exposed rock strata today. Over many millions of years, a rise of land known as an anticline was formed, on an axis extending from north to south. The high, exposed nature of this 'dome' (believed to have risen to a high point of 3,000 metres) meant that it was constantly subject to erosion by weathering, again over a long period of time. In the process, overlying rocks and the exposed upper layers of Coal Measures, shales and gritstone were worn away to reveal the underlying limestone. The high ground of the Millstone Grit, to the north, east and west sides of the dome, formed the Dark Peak. The limestone of the White Peak is the oldest rock of the Peak District and it is quite literally the bare bones of what was left after the erosion of the newer gritstones and shales.

Ice and Water Action

The Peak District was covered by ice during the Anglian glacial period (420,000 – 470,000 years ago). During the most recent Ice Age (Devensian 80,000 – 10,000 years ago) ice did not cover this area but local climatic conditions resembled the freezing tundra of present-day Siberia. The dynamic landscape forms associated with the gouging out of valleys by glaciers can be seen in the Scottish Highlands, the Lake District and Snowdonia. But the movement of ice through the Peak District was much more sluggish and our valleys and river systems were developed by the action of melt water and rock debris rather than glacial movement.

The effect of water on this landscape continues by chemical action. As rain falls, droplets absorb carbon dioxide, and as the rainwater filters through soil it becomes more concentrated with carbon dioxide, becoming in the process mildly acidic (carbonic acid). Over thousands of years this acid solution gradually permeates the limestone bedrock via fractures in the rock and dissolves the limestone away. Openings widen, fissures deepen, caves develop and complex underground drainage systems are formed.

Appendix 2: Mineral veins

Rakes are major veins that develop along extensive fractures in the limestone. They are big mineral-filled, vertical or sub-vertical cracks in the rock that may extend over a distance of some miles. One such is the Long Rake, a long, deep vein in the high limestone plateau, which is a fault line that runs across Middleton and Youlgrave Moor. Rakes have been mined to great depths of several hundred feet and are sometimes up to twenty feet wide. Shafts were sunk at intervals along the rake and spoil heaps were left at either side. This pattern of extraction is evident along the Long Rake, where mounds of earth and rock lie alongside the worked shaft. Extraction was achieved from 'stopes' (worked-out cavities) along horizontal levels that were reached from the vertical shaft.

Scrins are mini versions of rakes and sometimes break away from the major rakes. These veins are just one or two feet wide and go to a depth of around 200 feet. The old lead miners, who worked alone or in partnership, would often work these smaller veins and their spoil heaps look nowadays like interrupted chains of giant molehills or just regular bumps in the ground running in a line across a field.

Flats are mineral veins lying horizontally, often above a bed of toadstone, which is aligned with the predominantly flat-bedded limestone.

Pipes are cavities within the limestone that are rich with mineral deposits. These ancient caves are deep within the limestone strata but often alongside rakes. Miners were able to work into these caves from the shafts they had sunk into the rakes.

Appendix 3: Barmote Courts

The High Peak Barmote Court originally met at Monyash and the Low Peak Court met at Wirksworth. There were many Great Barmote Courts that met twice a year to swear in a new jury and to regulate major mining affairs. Youlgrave had its own Barmote Court. There were also Small Barmote Courts that met in the field to oversee day-to-day mining affairs or settle disputes.

The Great Courts, which consist of a Barmaster, a Steward and twelve jurors, continue to meet annually in April in the Moot Hall (the current one was built in 1814) in Wirksworth. While some of their activities are ceremonial, quarrying activity that involves the extraction of galena still comes under the scrutiny of the court. Two Parliamentary Acts were passed in the 1850s and confirmed that these courts were outside the jurisdiction of Common Law.

Appendix 4: Cupola Furnaces

In the cupola furnaces, the ore was not in direct contact with the fuel. Flames from burning coal were drawn across the ore by a carefully controlled draught supplied by long flues. A low arched roof on the furnace caused the flames to reverberate onto the ore so that the liquid metal was separated from the 'slag'. This sped up the smelting process and made it more efficient. The system was later refined by increasingly complex flue systems that condensed the fume, thereby containing some of the contaminants that had previously poisoned the land close by the smelting furnaces and, often, grazing stock. The products of the condensed fume were sometimes collected, but the main aim was to capture toxic material by cooling and condensing it. Sometimes this involved 'scrubbing' the fume with water sprayed through it.

The slag still contained valuable material that was often smelted again in a slag hearth, which would operate alongside the cupola smelting furnaces. The slag mills were water powered and so the newer smelting operations were often located near to a stream.

Appendix 5: Chalara Ash Dieback Disease (Chalara fraxinea)

The future appearance of the White Peak landscape hangs in the balance as we await the arrival of the Chalara Ash Dieback disease (Chalara fraxinea). This newly identified fungal disease has spread westwards, originating in Poland where it caused devastation to forests. It was identified in Britain in February 2012 in a consignment of infected nursery trees in Buckinghamshire that had come from the Netherlands. While the disease has been found in only one planted site in Derbyshire, it is finding its way into woodland all over Britain. There is infection in East Anglia and woodland areas along the eastern seaboard have been affected. Infection spreads by spores being carried on the wind. Forestry experts have calculated that this serious disease would take three seasons to reach the Peak District. Ash trees dominate Bradford Dale and all the other dales where they have colonised areas formerly dominated by elms. The best hope is that the ash woods of the dales may have some genetic variety that will prove resistant to the disease, but we won't know this for some years to come.

Appendix 6: Sustainable Youlgrave

Sustainable Youlgrave began in 2006 when a group of likeminded villagers in the Youlgrave area of the Derbyshire Peak District came together to discuss ways in which, by thinking globally but acting locally, they could do their bit to combat climate change and at the same time make their rural community more self-sufficient. The group has explored a range of initiatives covering renewable energy generation, including a £50,000 feasibility study into the possibilities of developing local anaerobic digestion (the breakdown of organic farmyard waste to create energy, fuel and improved fertiliser), as well as energy-saving and educational projects. These have included an energy survey of local public buildings, establishing a regular village market to dispose of allotment surplus and to promote local producers, creating new bee hives, and planting a community orchard. In 2007 Sustainable Youlgrave won the Community Group section of the national Future Friendly Awards. For more details go to: www.sustainableyoulgrave.org.

Little grebe

Mallard drake

Mute swan cygnet

Moorhen with chick

Acknowledgements

This book would not exist without the support and expertise of members of the Bradford River Action Group (BRAG): Fred Baker, Dave Brown, Pat Coleman, Maggie Ford, Jo Hepper, Andrew McCloy, Nicky Philips, Warren Slaney and Geoff Williams. *A River in Time* was collectively initiated and inspired by the group who are behind the celebration of the River Bradford and who have met often to provide feedback and advice. BRAG members have given huge amounts of their time freely and made strenuous efforts to ensure the success of the whole of this project.

Many local people from Middleton, Youlgrave and Alport shared their memories and thoughts about the river with me. Thanks to residents Don Bateman, Henry and Eileen Brocklehurst, John Folley and Margaret Folley, Lillian Oldfield, Anthony Wragg and Chris Wragg, whose words bring the recent past back to life on these pages. Thanks also to members of the Youlgrave Waterworks Committee, Gordon Coupe, Eric Goodwin and Malcolm Stacey who outlined the vital work that they do and special thanks to Gordon who let me reproduce two of his wonderful collection of old postcards. Also thanks to John Youatt for his comments and the photo of the Middleton Corn Mill and to Charles Monkhouse for the Derbyshire map.

Special thanks to Joy Frost for her feedback and enthusiasm over many months and for putting me on some of the better tracks.

I am indebted to various people who generously shared their knowledge and expertise in guiding a novice through entirely new territory. I wish to thank Dr Bob Toynton who patiently helped me towards a rudimentary understanding of the geology of the Derbyshire Dales and for his reading of many drafts; Dr Trevor Ford who has kindly proof read and advised and whose geological sections are included in the book; also Geoff Williams who made helpful suggestions on the geology and hydrology of the area and Dr Jim Rieuwerts who read Part 3 closely and helped with both information and comments. Thanks also to Lyn Willies for kind access to his photographic collection and to Dickie Bird for his permission to use his stunning underground images. Thanks to Mary Bartlett who read and commented on text relating to monastic settlement. Special thanks to Warren Slaney, Head River Keeper for the Haddon Estate who accompanied me along the Bradford and whose illuminating ideas and observations form much of the text of Part 4.

Several officers at the Peak District National Park Authority have given support, advice and documents. I am especially grateful to Richard Godley who has supported this project from the earliest stages and helped us to secure the funding, Rhodri Thomas who read Part 2 with great care and who enriched this section with details on many of the botanical treasures to be found along the Bradford, and thanks to Karen Shelley-Jones for her input on and photographs of white-clawed crayfish. I would also like to thank staff at the Derbyshire Local Studies Library in Matlock for their advice and assistance. Thanks to Isabella Stone from Friends of the Peak District for her feedback and support. Thanks to Ruth Headon and to Lord Edward Manners for providing access to the eighteenth-century Haddon Estate maps, some of which are reproduced and all of which proved useful in unravelling aspects of the river's past.

My thanks to Lindy Payling at Grafika for her excellent design work, and endless patience in much shuffling of text and pictures, to Chris Eaton for his initial design concept, James Bettney for his photographs of the Haddon maps and to Mark Ramsden for his enthusiastic support in overseeing the project at Grafika, and making this publication possible. Also thanks to Nicola Ball

for her final and vital proof reading and to Patricia Stubbs for her close reading and editing of early drafts.

A huge thank-you to Lord Chris Smith for taking the time to read through this book and providing such a valuable and thoughtful foreword.

Thanks to my friends and family (especially Doug, Nicky, Bill and Diana) who have given me much-needed moral support over the months of writing and compiling. A big thanks to my daughter Lucy who has illuminated many things for me both geographical and climatalogical and who is, so often, right. Finally thanks to my partner Tony Mead who has lived with this book for a year, has endlessly re-read the text, made many suggestions over source material, and whose encouragement and enthusiasm I could not have done without.

Christine Gregory

Bibliography

Ardley, B. and Bartlett, M. The Spirit of Youlgrave and Alport. Landmark Publishing Ltd, 2003.

Arkwright Society (1974). Local history Trail No 15, Youlgreave, Middleton, Alport.

Barnatt, B. and Penny, R. The Lead Legacy. Peak District National Park Authority, English Heritage and English Nature, 2004.

Barrett, D. An Archaeological Resource Assessment of Medieval Derbyshire. Derbyshire County Council.

Bates, T. (2007). 'The Rivers Bradford and Lathkill'. Peak District Online.

Bunting, J. Bygone Industries of the Peak. Wildtrack Publishing, 2006.

Census records for Youlgrave, 1841.

Coupe, G. Youlgrave: A Southern Peakland Village. University of Sheffield,1993.

Culshaw, G. (August 2009). 'Life and Death in the 19th Century'. Family Tree Magazine, 32-34.

Dalton, R., Fox, H. and Jones, P. Classic Landforms of the White Peak. Geographical Association in conjunction with British Geomorphological Research Group, 1987, (1999 edn).

Daniel, M. (1982). 'The Origin of the Barmote Court System: A New Theory'. Bulletin of the Peak District Mines Historical Society, Vol. 8, No. 3.

Defoe, D. A Tour Thro' the Whole Island of Great Britain. 1724 – 27.

Derbyshire Archaeological Journal. 'Population in Derbyshire in the reign of Charles 2nd', 117.

Dodd, A. E. and Dodd, E. M. Peakland Roads and Trackways. Landmark Publishing Ltd, 3rd Edition 2000.

Drury, C. 'Historic Youlgrave' published in A Sheaf of Essays, Northend, 1929.

English Heritage (1996). Extract from Record of Scheduled Monuments: Alport Smelt Mill.

Environment Agency (2012). 'Rivers Bradford and Lathkill'.

Environment Agency. 'Native White-clawed Crayfish'.

Ford, T. D. Rocks and Scenery of the Peak District, Landmark Publishing, 2002.

Ford, T. D. (2004). 'Geology of the Lead mines Around the Stanton Syncline'. Bulletin of the Peak District Mines Historical Society, Vol. 15, No. 6.

Ford, T. D. and Rieuwerts, J.H. (Ed) Lead Mining in the Peak District, 3rd Edition Peak Park Joint Planning Board and Peak District Mines Historical Society,1983 and 4th Edition revised and expanded, Landmark Publishing for P.D.M.H.S., 2000.

Glover, S. The History, Gazeteer and Directory of the County of Derby, Longman, 1829.

Harvey, F. (10 June 2011). 'England sees driest spring in a century as drought hits UK', Guardian.

Hodges, R. Wall-to-Wall History: The Story of Roystone Grange. Duckworth, 1991.

Holderness, H., Davies, G., Chamberlain, A. and Donahue, R. Research Report: A Conservation Audit of Archaeological Cave Resources in the Peak District and Yorkshire Dales. Archaeological Research and Consultancy at the University of Sheffield (ARCUS) for English Heritage, Jan 2006.

Hughes, T. River – Poems by Ted Hughes. Faber and Faber, 1983.

Joint Nature Conservation Committee. 'Invertebrate Species: arthropods: White-clawed (or Atlantic Stream) Crayfish'. jncc.defra.gov.uk.

Last, J. (2011). 'Prehistoric Henges and Circles', English Heritage.

Llewellyn Jewitt F. S. A. (Ed). The Reliquary – Quarterly Archeological Journal and Review, John Russell Smith 1863 – 64.

Lovegrove, R. Silent Fields: The Long Decline of a Nation's Wildlife, Oxford University Press, 2007.

McBhride, F. (April 1999). ' The application of archaeological theory to the study of 'Celtic' water cults, with particular reference to holy wells studies'.

McCloy, A. and Wilson, N. The Mawstone Mine Disaster, Bugle, 2007.

McKie, R. (3 March 2013). 'Droughts and Floods "will be common events in Britain" ', The Observer.

Middleton Village History Group. Our Middleton: An historical celebration of the ancient parish of Middleton and Smerill, 2001.

Mosley, M. (2013). '50 Great British Inventions', Radio Times, BBC.

Nature Conservancy Council/British Geological Survey. Regionally Important Geological and Geomorphological Sites (RIGS). RIGS proposal: Alport Tufa (1992). RIGS proposal: Bradford Dale (1993). RIGS proposal: Rhienstor Rock (1993).

Natural England. 'Water Voles', www.naturalengland.org.uk.

Natural England (2008). Exploratory Memorandum to the Wildlife and Countryside Act 1981 (Variation of Schedule 5) (England). www.naturalengland.org.uk.

Naylor, P. J. Ancient Wells and Springs of Derbyshire, Scarthin Books, 1983.

Naylor, P. (1995). 'Two Old Miners', Bulletin of the Peak District Mines Historical Society, Vol. 12, No. 5.

Ordnance Survey. Derbyshire 1896 –1900. DA (Digital Archives).

Ordnance Survey. Touring Map and Guide: Peak District. Scale One inch to One Mile, 1995.

Ordnance Survey. Buxton and Matlock. 1:50 000 Landranger Map 119, 2006.

Ordnance Survey. The Peak District, White Peak Area. 1:25 000 Explorer Map 24, 2004.

Parker Stamper, W. Youlgrave - A Derbyshire Village, first published B. Gratton 1902, republished A. Scrivener, 1988.

Peak District National Park Authority. Adapting to Climate Change in the Peak District National Park, PDNPA, September 2011.

Peak District National Park Authority, Peak District Landscape Character Assessment (Landscape Strategy and Action Plan) 2: White Peak, PDNPA, July 2009.

Peak District National Park Authority, A Living landscape – Biodiversity Action Plan for the Peak District (White-clawed Crayfish), PDNPA and Natural England, 2012.

Peak District National Park Authority (2012). 'Wetland Species', PDNPA.

Peak District National Park Authority. Alport Conservation Area Appraisal, PDNPA, February 2012.

Peak District National Park Authority. Youlgrave Conservation Area Appraisal, PDNPA, August 2010.

Radley, J. (1963). 'Peak District Roads prior to the Turnpike Era'. The Derbyshire Archeological Journal, Issue 83, 39-50.

Randerson, J. (29 December 2008). 'Breeding Programme boosts endangered crayfish species'. Guardian.

Reuters (Monday 3 December 2012). 'CO$_2$ emission rises mean climate change now almost certain'. Guardian.co.uk.

Rieuwerts, J.H. Glossary of Derbyshire Lead Mining Terms, PDMHS Ltd, 1998.

Robson, L. A Gazeteer of the White Peak, J.H. Hall and Sons Ltd, 1991.

Shaw, R.P. (2002). 'Arbor Low Calcite Mine, Youlgrave, Derbyshire', The Bulletin of the Peak District Mines Historical Society, Vol. 15, No. 1.

Shaw, R. P. (1995). 'Long Rake Spar Mine' The Bulletin of the Peak District Mines Historical Society', Vol. 12, No. 5.

Shelley-Jones, K. Project Report, Crayfish Arks. PDNPA, March 2011.

Shimwell, J.W. (1984). 'History of Youlgrave and its People'.

Smith, R. 'Prehistory of the Peak', www.peakdistrict-nationalpark.com.

Southern, R.W. Western Society and the Church in the Middle Ages, Penguin, 1970.

Thompson, E.P. The Making of the English Working Class, 2nd edition, Penguin, 1968.

Turner, S. (2000). 'Aspects of the development of public assembly in the Danelaw'. Department of Archaeology, University of York.

Waller, J. The Real Oliver Twist, Icon Books Ltd, 2005.

Walton, I. The Compleat Angler, 1653.

White, F. History and Gazeteer of Derbyshire, 1857.

Willies, L. (1999). 'Derbyshire Lead Mining in the 18th and 19th centuries', Bulletin of the Peak District Mines Historical Society, Vol. 14, No. 2.

Willies, L. (1990). 'Derbyshire Lead Smelting in the 18th and 19th centuries', Bulletin of the Peak District Mines Historical Society, Vol. III, No 1.

Willies, L. (1983). 'The Barker Family and Wyatt Lead Mining Businesses, 1730 – 1875'. Bulletin of the Peak District Mines Historical Society, Vol.8, No.3.

Wilson, G.N. The Tap Dressers – A Celebration, Country Books, 2000.

Youlgrave Women's Institute. Some account of Youlgrave, Middleton and Alport, 1931.

Christine Gregory

is a writer, photographer and painter. She has lived in the Derbyshire Dales since 1990, exploring it extensively and developing a close understanding of its natural history.

Her book on hares, *Brown Hares in the Derbyshire Dales* was first published in 2010 after several years of following, studying and photographing these iconic animals. A second edition was published in 2012 with sixty new photographs. The book came out of a life-long love of the countryside and concern for the environment.

Having taught social and political studies in adult and community education for more than 20 years of the first part of her career, she went on to teach radio skills and print journalism in further education. She has made community-based radio programmes for BBC Radio Sheffield and features for Radio 4, but now concentrates full-time on writing, photography and painting.

www.christinegregory.co.uk

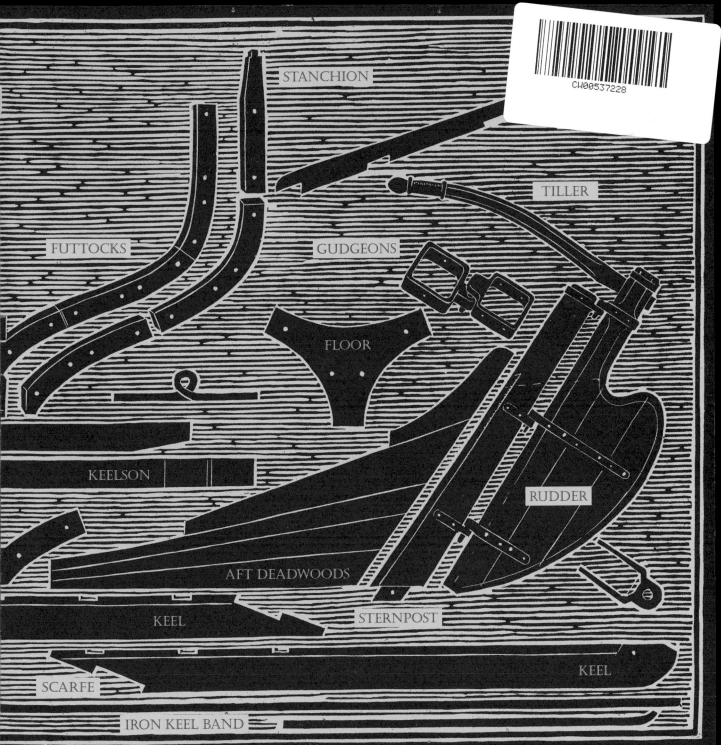

STANCHION

TILLER

FUTTOCKS

GUDGEONS

FLOOR

KEELSON

RUDDER

AFT DEADWOODS

KEEL

STERNPOST

KEEL

SCARFE

IRON KEEL BAND

the song of the
WATERLILY

the building of a boat

the song of the
WATERLILY

the building of a boat

Newell
&
Dodds

Jardine Press Ltd

These paintings and linocuts are based on the
rebuilding of the Essex deep sea smack "Pioneer"
to which this book is dedicated.

The Pioneer now works as a sail training vessel
which, along with the Pioneer Training School
helps to keep alive the skills of the Maritime Trades.

Text © Martin Newell 2003
Images © James Dodds 2003
Designed by Catherine Clark
lst edition Jardine Press Ltd 2003
2nd edition Jardine Press Ltd 2008
ISBN 978 0 9552035 7 2
www.jardinepress.co.uk
www.pioneersailingtrust.org.uk

LIST OF ILLUSTRATIONS

COVER AND TITLE PAGE:
Bow of a Smack *(Oil on Linen)*

THE SONG OF THE PARTS:
First Futtocks Raised *(Linocut)*
In Frame *(2 Colour Linocut)*
Looking Aft *(Oil on Linen)*
Planking *(2 Colour Linocut)*
Looking Forward *(Oil on Linen)*
Deck Beams *(2 Colour Linocut)*
Aft Futtock Frames *(Woodcut)*

THE SHIPWRIGHT'S SONG:
Midship Section with Wet Well Bulkheads *(Oil on Linen)*
Adzing the Mast *(Linocut)*
Fore Bulkhead *(Oil on Linen)*
Caulking the Decks *(Linocut)*
Aft Bulkhead *(Oil on Linen)*

THE SONG OF THE STORM:
On the Slipway Ready to Launch *(Linocut)*
On the Hard *(Linocut)*
At Sea (detail) *(Linocut)*
Storm *(Linocut)*

THE LAST SONG:
Bow *(Oil on Linen)*
Stern *(Oil on Linen)*

INTRODUCTION

Even those who have not had the joy of spending time at sea are likely to agree that a chain is as strong as its weakest link. Unlike the television series that rejects the weakest, the seafaring tradition forges links and builds strength. Seafarers know that this kind of teamwork is essential at sea, an uncompromising environment, where lives literally depend upon it. This powerful principle of interdependence extends to inanimate parts of the ship that are hidden from view: for example, the piston, unseen, drives the ship nonetheless.

We have much to learn from these maritime ideas. In a culture ashore that is sometimes more fluent on rights than focused on responsibilities, we can learn from those at sea how much it matters that each member of a crew is equally important, how each element of the ship must take a share of the strain. I was often reminded of this during my time in the Royal Navy, where as the Captain of the aircraft carrier *Invincible*, I depended, for instance, upon more than a thousand people to pull their weight before each Sea Harrier was launched on a mission.

Now, in Greenwich, I am conscious that our stimulating range of exhibitions, conferences, books, websites and shows depends upon the teamwork of hundreds. Each person has to play his or her part to ensure that we can all take pride in a result that attracts and informs our public, as we "illustrate the importance of the sea, ships, time and the stars".

The Song of the Waterlily describes the unity of a ship in a storm; the message is one of significance for us all as we navigate the rough waters of life. Martin Newell has written an evocative poem that is illustrated appropriately by James Dodds, whose images have the happy knack of capturing the essence and atmosphere of seafaring. His work is on show around Britain and we in Greenwich are looking forward especially to his exhibition *Shipshape* at the National Maritime Museum.

Roy Clare
Director, National Maritime Museum, Greenwich, February 2003

SONG OF THE WATERLILY

From keel and keelson,
strakes and sails

From floors and decking
up to mast

We'll pull together stem to stern
We are the ship, a ship at last.

We'll pull together, pull together
Any weather sky can cast

Pull together, stem to stern
We are the ship, a ship at last.

THE SONG OF THE PARTS

A wooden boat, un-named, untried
Lies moored and waiting for the tide
With maiden voyage due next day
A light wind ushers night away.
As if to praise the shipwright's arts
A hubbub rises from her parts
As one by one, each sings its song
To prove the previous singer wrong:

"I am The Keel, therefore the king
For me, the adze and whetstone sing
To shape me, scarve me for my reign
Along the length of my demesne
I am the strength, I am the spine
The spirit of the ship is mine
And hewn from woodland oak so tall
Take precedence above you all."

"I am The Stem I rule the bow
The Keel will kneel before me now
And once I'm hoisted into place
Let no-one claim a stronger case
Apart perhaps, from just one other
Since I have a distant brother
In The Sternpost whom you'll see
Located to the aft of me.

Stem and Sternpost, stern and stem
The Keel depends on both of them
Between us both, the reign is halved
The Stern is tenoned, Stem is scarved
But nonetheless these dual kings
Shall rule above all other things
And every lowly plank and wale
Shall pay us tribute when we sail."

"We are The Deadwoods, timber blocks
Who help insure against such shocks
The previous kings may not withstand
Despite pretensions of being grand
And while they are affixed to us
They have no right to boast, discuss
Their sovereignty above the rest
Until their strength is put to test."

"We are The Floors – of old, The Flowers
Those timbers which retain the powers
To be the proving of this boat
And all who sail her, once afloat.
So here across the keel we lie
The shipwright's hammer standing by
Must clench us, Keel and Keelson, in
Before all other jobs begin."

"I am The Keelson, king-to-be
The Keel is weak, deprived of me
I'm like my father, made of joints
And scarved – although at different points
I am the power behind his throne
He'd break, were he to reign alone
If not for all this work I do
So though I'm hidden, I reign too."

"We are The Futtocks, ribs are we
To brace the planking 'gainst the sea
From ancient oak, its branches chained,
We're cut to shape. The strakes constrained
By our full strength, provide the shield
From any blow the storm may wield
While laying siege to breech the wood
Without our help, the boat's no good."

"We are The Planks, The Strakes and Wales
No ship that sailed – or ever sails
Can do so till we're fitted in
To help provide her with her skin
The sheer-strake first and then the rest
Once plied to shape in steaming chest
Are lifted, fitted, spiked in place
To give the finished craft its grace."

"We are The Deckbeams, in a storm
We help preserve the vessel's form
We're laid athwartships, once we're down
The Decking then shall be our gown
For men to work and walk upon
The cygnet now becomes a swan.
Without us at the vessel's hub
The ship would merely be a tub."

"I am The Oakum, humble stuff
From hemp or jute, a greasy fluff
Of fibres, forced into the gaps
Between the planks, by mallet taps
I'm sealed with pitch until just right
To make the vessel watertight
The boat's no use to anyone
If caulkyer's work is left undone."

"We are The Sails and The Mast
And though we may be fitted last
We catch all winds to make our slaves
And push the boat across the waves
The master Mast, holds Sail, the dame
With chest puffed out, she'll justly claim
Without her ballet in the air
The boat will languish, drifting there."

"All very well!" The Tiller creaks
The Rudder cricking, as he speaks:
"A pretty pas-de-deux my dear.
Yet pointless, if you cannot steer
The wind's your master not your slave
And can't be trusted to behave
Since once the vessel is afloat,
It's we two parts control this boat."

And now the parts had had their say
Unproved and quiet the new ship lay
While carpenters and riggers came
Her owners pondered on a name
With maiden voyage looming up
They drink a toast. Her christening cup
Is drained until the liquor's gone
And Waterlily settled on.

THE SHIPWRIGHT'S SONG

"I'll sweep the floor, I'll make the tea, and then
I'll sweep the floor and sweep the floor again
Shall I?" apprentice mutters to himself
His master shuffles papers on the shelf.
Draws up dimensions, costs and thinks of wood
The work and care required to make her good
This boat which he and Tommy must begin
As Summer ebbs away and days draw in.

The trees arrive, the oak to make the keel
Spare men come in, lend shoulders to the wheel
And when the lorry and the men depart
Old Chris and his apprentice make a start
And to the sawpit, trees and shipwrights go
The senior man above, the boy below
For ripped and splintered days with no abate
With muscles taxed at source – and at top rate.

A week of this, the boy balks at his chore
He wonders if his arms can take much more
New-hardened hands so numb they barely feel
The two commence construction of the keel
Their adzes sharpened fine enough to split
A penny, heads-from-tails with one smart hit.
They'll make and lay the keel into its bed
Where blocks have been put down, inside the shed.

Now Tommy takes the tool, begins to work
Old Chris looks on and tells him with a smirk:
"Stop taking beeswings off boy, get it right
Or else we'll both be here till Christmas night."
The boy's still ginger but the master sees
His swing becomes more steady by degrees
And as the days wear on, more steady still
He gleans a fraction of the old man's skill.

With mornings colder now and time got past
The keelson and the floors bolt in at last
"A tricky job," says Chris and Tommy aches
From clenching, and the hammering it takes
The older man impatient and in pain
Back-ache, old injuries, play up again
If Tommy moans, Chris snaps: "You needn't fear.
It's just young muscles clicking into gear."

Now Chris shows Tommy how the futtocks go
Cut out from oak, grown eight-score year ago
Not forest oak, but hedgerow oak – the bends
And crooks of branches suited for such ends –
To fashion what will be the ribs inside
And later still, the planks and wales will hide
And which, once they've been fitted and are on
Will show the boat – at least its skeleton.

The deadwoods must be trimmed, rabbets connected
The oak and elm for planking be inspected
For deadknots, shakes or any bit gone bad
Before they make the strakes and ship is clad
Time comes for planking up – to help with this,
Another pair of shipwrights, asked by Chris
Come in to help as new-steamed planks, still warm
Are fitted, spiked and thus, a boat takes form.

The days are darker now and dashed with rain
The adze, the maul, the hammer and the plane
Will echo in the dwindling winter light
And Tommy feels he's working more by night
The decking planks go down and bit by bit
Chris shows the young apprentice how they'll fit
And tells him, " . . . with such little space to spare,
You couldn't get a fag paper in there."

The work continues, Christmas comes and goes
And in the yard a sickle east wind blows
Which slices through the shed, along the floor
Where Tommy opens oakum bales once more
Regards the greasy floss, hands digging in
The caulking of the decks will now begin
And tappings from his mallet will provide
A rhythm to the howling gales outside.

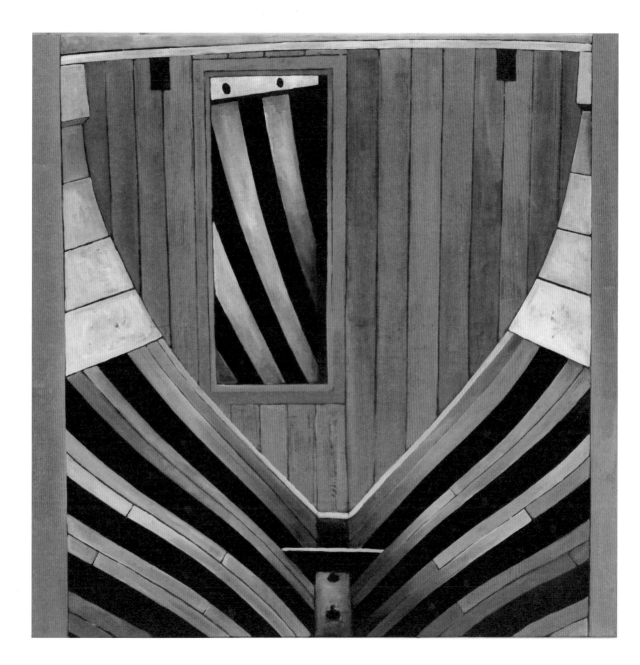

Then over months with oakum, pitch and paint
The savvy, skill, the patience of a saint
Chris teases out a shipwright from the lad
Sands up the good and planes away the bad
Till Winter slings his hook and leaves the shed
And Spring stands beaming on the yard instead
Then extra hands are once again called back
Since now, it's time to launch the finished smack.

Finished though it's not, just halfway through
And after launch there'll still be work to do
As much as in the days already passed
The standing rigging, ballast, sails, mast
The running rigging, mast hoop, gaff and boom
And this will leave the shipwrights little room
To rest upon such laurels as they've earned
Though Tommy can proud of what he's learned.

And most of all he won't forget the day
The ship slips slowly down the greasy way
The skids well-packed with tallow, grease and fat
An empty space left where the boat had sat
"She floats. She really floats!" exclaims the boy.
The older shipwright grins to see his joy.
With cheers and sheer excitement in the air
A ship she is, the Waterlily there.

WE ARE THE SHIP (SHANTY)

From keel and keelson,
strakes and sails

From floors and decking
up to mast

We'll pull together stem to stern
We are the ship, a ship at last.

We'll pull together, pull together
Any weather sky can cast

Pull together, stem to stern
We are the ship, a ship at last.

THE SONG OF THE STORM

Regatta eve, slack-water, still
A smoky low September chill
Which loiters in the river air
Accosts the Waterlily there
Where misty skeins around her sails
Hang lacier than bridal veils
As if to hide her sleeping face.
Tomorrow is her maiden race.

A crew. A crew? The best we've got.
All filched from fishing boat and yacht
Handpicked the lot – and Essexmen.
Each man as good as any ten
A lesser county might yield up.
The challenge, money and the cup
Are good as theirs. Already won
Before they hear the starter gun.

Regatta day, the Colneside din:
"Lee-oh!" The tiller round and in.
The Waterlily trimmed at last
Her ballast right, her brand new mast
She handles well – or round about
Allowing it's her first time out.
And second in, they bring her back
A veteran – an Essex smack.

Triumphant home to quay she comes
To cheerful crowds and booming drums
And bands which play all afternoon
Her sea trials done, the work starts soon
For Waterlily though, her crew
Have far more pressing things to do
Regatta night comes once a year
Lord help them they should wait for beer.

A scant week on, the autumn sky
Has filled, the leaden clouds scull by
The breezes rag the flags about
The halliards rattle rhythms out
And Waterlily, on the quay
Is fitted now for work at sea
She waits as crew take on supplies
And skipper stands, surveying the skies.

The waves kick up, the west wind sings
To Winter waiting in the wings
And morning tide is high, the ship
Is girded for her working trip
The crew and skipper light of heart
With fair-to-goodish wind to start
North east across the sea she heads
To Terschelling and oyster-beds.

It's here the Waterlily dredges.
Winding up her hoeing edges.
Aching muscles, shredded hands
Added to what catch she lands
Help her crew to comprehend
Which are the means and what the end
In case they'd reason to confuse
Their voyage with a pleasure cruise.

And yet the work, though never light
Goes smoother than perhaps it might
The grey-flecked North Sea days go past
Till oysters fill the hold at last
And with a wind that's scarce a breeze
A milky sun and eerie seas
Such halcyon conditions reign
The skillinger heads home again.

For hours, the Waterlily drifts
In wind so light she barely shifts
The oddly balmy air feels warm
But further west, dark shadows form
And sun is lava, raw red light
A flux which solders day to night
The wind turns colder, changing tack
And brings the rain in on its back.

Then rapidly, the glass gets low
The vessel reefed, awaits a blow
That when it comes, is of a strength
To thresh the bulwark down its length
Shattering almost half the rail
While in the whining of the gale
The echoes in the timbers sing:
"I am the Keel – therefore the king."

A hollow sound, which dies away
A swansong from another day
Till one-by-one for their own sakes
The keel, the keelson, floors and strakes
United by the tempest now
Become as one, from stern to bow
And sing against the deadly weather
"We are the ship. We pull together."

And so the song of all the parts
This proofing of the shipwright's arts
Comes through above the keening gale
And while the timber, or the sail
May sing convincing verses for us
None is stirring as the chorus
Rendered when in troubled weather
Now they learn to pull together.

Amid leviathan waves, the smack
Is dwarfed, she plunges, battling back.
Her timbers creak and in her hold
The hapless crew are hurled and rolled
Their locker seats and clothing wet
The barrels, butts and lamps upset
But still their doughty fishing boat
The Waterlily, stays afloat.

For hours it blows, without remorse.
The skipper strives to hold her course
And tied near tiller, there he'll stay
Till night gives, grudging, in to day.
The wind abates, the gales subside
The crew awaits and prays the tide
Is favourable – or fair at least
As wind whips round from north to east.

Then with this breeze to catch her sail
And wood to fix her broken rail
Her crew will patch her up somehow
While Waterlily rallies now
Within the sight of Saxon shore
The same her predecessors saw
Carved out and planed by restless seas
Down centuries of days like these.

And in she glides to port at last
From curve of keel to tip of mast
A working ship, in stern and bow
And no-one can reproach her now
Or say her workmanship was bad
Her fish-hold full and crew so glad
They're safely home, they never see
The shipwrights waiting on the quay . . .

SONG OF THE WATERLILY

From keel and keelson,
strakes and sails

From floors and decking
up to mast

We'll pull together stem to stern
We are the ship, a ship at last.

We'll pull together, pull together
Any weather sky can cast

Pull together, stem to stern
We are the ship, a ship at last.

THE LAST SONG

Beneath a wild and wind-torn autumn sky
The shipwrights watch their handiwork limp by
The older man is lost in calculation
Of wood for her repair – plus preparation
Regards the damage done by all the gales
Remembers the dimensions of her rails
Yet, proud his work survived in such a blow
Stands on the quay bathed in the afterglow.

Young Tommy sees the Waterlily's crew
Dock in, and start those chores still left to do
A fisherman his age looks up to shout:
"It got us there and back – well, just about!"
He grins at Tommy as he jumps ashore:
"I ain't convinced she's up to any more."
But as the boy approaches, Tommy spies
The sheer relief there, lurking in his eyes.

The sundry cuts and bruises crewmen sport
Provide the shipwrights with the sober thought
That skill at building ships was all there'd be
To stand between the sailor and the sea
And Tommy wonders if he'd sail in one
Enquiring of the worst trip Chris had done
But Chris replies: "Worst trip? I never go.
Don't sail 'em. I just build the things, you know."

From keel and keelson,
Strakes and sails

From floors and decking
up to mast

We'll pull together, stem to stern
We are the ship, a ship at last.

We'll pull together, pull together
Any weather sky can cast

Pull together, stem to stern
We are the ship.

A ship at last.

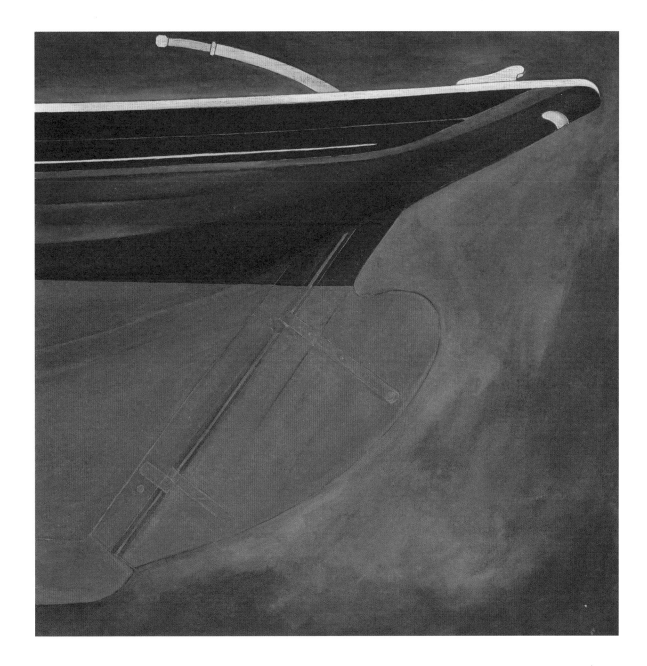

FINAL WORD

I had to study very hard to write these verses, since when I started I knew barely anything about the building or sailing of fishing smacks. My friend James Dodds, who was a shipwright before he became an artist, was my chief educator. Long hours were spent plying him with questions about technicalities and terminology. Reams of archive photostats arrived on my desk. Cassette and video tapes from suitably maritime sources were consumed. Piles of books came from James' substantial collection. As fast as I returned a volume read, another would turn up. There were times when I thought that the subject would take over my life.

Aside from these studies, there was a field trip. After I'd learned what the parts of a ship were called and what they did, James drove me over to Scripps Farm at Great Totham, where the old Class 1 deep-sea fishing smack, the *Pioneer*, was being restored. I spent some time looking around the craft and observing what happens in a shipyard. Around this time, at the age of 49, I also learned to row. This helped me to explore the River Colne and to understand it in a way which would be impossible merely from its shores.

The books and texts I most often referred to were: Ted Frost's *From Tree To Sea*, C.W.T. Layton's *Dictionary Of Nautical Words And Terms*, John Leather's *The Northseamen* and one or two related articles from nautical magazines – most notably Hazell White's article, *The Brightlingsea Dredger-men*. For sheer atmosphere, I read William Golding's *Rites Of Passage* and listened to various sea shanties and poems from the past two centuries.

Not everything I've learned has gone into my verses. There simply wasn't room. I hope however that the salient things about building, launching and sailing a fishing smack have been adequately and atmospherically portrayed within these poems. It was the single hardest poetry project I've ever had to complete. I hope I've done it well, because another thing which I've learned during my studies, is that many nautical types tend to be scrupulously accurate about what they say, write and do. I hesitate to draw a cannonade from them for slipshod work.

The simplest thing I can say about fishing smacks, their construction and sailing is that it's a very humbling thing for a landsman such as myself to understand even roughly, as I now do, what goes into the making and sailing of these boats. I live in an age where a man may sit on a chair and not know how it's built, or drink a pint of beer and not know how it's brewed. For me to learn how a boat is built – a boat which can put food on tables and keep its crew safe from the sea – has been an education. I hope I can pass something of it back to the reader.

Martin Newell

GLOSSARY OF TERMS

Adze:	Sharp-bladed shipwright's tool with curved handle for chopping away surplus wood, similar to an axe.
Aft/ Abaft:	Towards the stern of a ship.
Athwartships:	Transversely across a ship: across-ways.
Ballast:	Heavy substances (lumps of stone or metal) put into boat to improve stability.
"Beeswings":	Skimpy wood-shavings taken by overly timid use of the adze.
Bitts:	Strong vertical posts through the deck that secure the windlass and the bowsprit.
Boom:	A spar having jaws that fit round the mast, which secures the foot of the mainsail.
Bow:	The part of the ship that extends aft and downwards of its stem.
Bowsprit:	Horizontal spar projecting from the vessel's bow.
Bulwark:	Wooden sides around outboard edge of deck to protect deck from seas.
Carling:	A fore and aft deck beam.
Caulking:	Making joints watertight by tapping lengths of oakum into the gaps.
Clenching:	Shipwright's technique of fixing a bolt through two or more wooden objects after which the end of the bolt is beaten flat to secure it, from "clinched".
Counter:	Sloping underside of the hull aft of the sternpost and above the waterline.
Deadwoods:	Flat vertical surfaces at junction of stem or sternpost with keel.
Deck Beam:	Strong beams across the vessel to support the deck and help preserve the vessel's shape.
Floors:	Vertical transverse members which connect lower ends of frames on opposite sides of vessel crossing the keel.
Futtocks:	The ribs or frames of a wooden vessel (foot hooks).
Gaff:	A spar having jaws that fit round the mast, which secures the head of the mainsail.
Greasy Way:	The rails or skids packed with grease which a boat is sent down at launching.
Halcyon:	A bird (kingfisher) said by the ancients to favour nesting at sea during a period of calm warm days surrounding the winter solstice. Hence: halcyon days.
Halliards:	Running rigging. Ropes by which gaffs, sails or flags are hoisted.
Hanging Knee:	Vertical knee under the deck beams.
Hoeing Edges:	The edges of the nets used in dredging for oysters, scraping the sea floor.
Horn Timber:	Fore and aft timber that forms the backbone of the counter.
Hove To:	When the jib is backed and the mainsail holds the boat steady almost into the wind.
Keel:	Lowest and main part of ship's construction. The spine of the ship.
Keel Bolts:	Bolts which hold the keelson, floors and keel together.
Keelson:	Internal keel, fitted above the keel and floors for increased strength.
"Lee-oh!":	Said by the helmsman to alert the crew that he is about to change course by moving the tiller so that the vessel turns through the eye of the wind.
Leviathan:	A sea monster.
Lodging Knee:	A knee or bend horizontal between the deck beams.
Mast Hoop:	Circular ring of metal or wood encircling a mast, free to move up and down it.

Maul:	Type of large hammer used by shipwrights.
Oakum:	Hemp or jute rope which has been unpicked then proofed with oil for use in caulking.
Planks:	Lengths of timber more than nine inches across, used for sides or skin of boat.
Rabbetts:	Cutaways or rebates in stem, deadwoods, keel and sternpost for planks to fit into.
Rail:	Top of bulwarks.
Reefing:	Reducing area of a sail by gathering it in at certain points.
Rudder:	Paddle-like piece of wood at stern, used for steering.
Running Rigging:	All ropes rove through blocks and worked as necessary, moveable rather than standing rigging.
Saxon Shore:	Coastline (from 6th century on) of southern England and East Anglia.
Scarve:	Wooden joint with bevelled ends, used when uniting two ends of planks.
Shakes:	Faults or flaws in timber caused in felling or by storm damage.
Sheer-strake:	The main top plank or strake in a vessel's side.
Shrouds:	Stays of rope or wire rigging the braces the mast.
Skids:	The rough greased rails of a greasy way used at launching.
Skillinger:	Type of deep sea fishing smack built in North Essex in 19th century. Corruption of Terschellinger.
Slack Water:	Of a tidal river: a short period when the tide is turning and the water seems still.
Smack:	Fishing vessel.
Spiked:	Shipwrighting term for nailed.
Spiling:	Transferring the curved shape of a part of a boat to a flat piece of wood, using a template or mould.
Stanchion:	The uppermost futtock extending through the deck to form the bulwarks and rails.
Standing Rigging:	Shrouds, forestay, backstays etc. Fixed rigging. As opposed to running rigging.
Steaming:	Planks are steamed to render them more pliable for fitting to the frame of a ship.
Stem:	Piece of wood rising upwards from fore end of keel which it is scarved or tenoned into the keel.
Sternpost:	Vertical piece of wood at aft end of ship and tenoned into the aft of the keel.
Strake:	Line of planking along length of ship from forward to aft.
Tallow:	Substance made from harder types of animal fat for grease or candles etc.
Tenon:	Type of carpentry joint consisting of projecting piece of wood fitted into cavity (mortise) on corresponding piece of wood. Mortise and tenon.
Terschelling:	Dutch island off Friesian coast which lent its name to the oyster grounds of that name.
Tiller:	Lever at head of rudder which ship is steered by.
Trenail:	or Trunnel. A wooden peg or nail.
Trimming:	Adjusting. Applies to sails for instance, where they're trimmed for best efficiency for the direction in which the vessel wishes to sail according to the wind direction.
Wales:	The thickest and strongest strakes in the hull of a wooden ship. Inwales or beamshelf inside the boat.
Well:	Wet well. A flooded compartment to keep alive caught fish and shell fish.
Whetstone:	Shaped stone for sharpening tools, often lubricated with oil.
Windlass:	A horizontal capstan attached by bearings to the bitts, for hauling up the anchor.

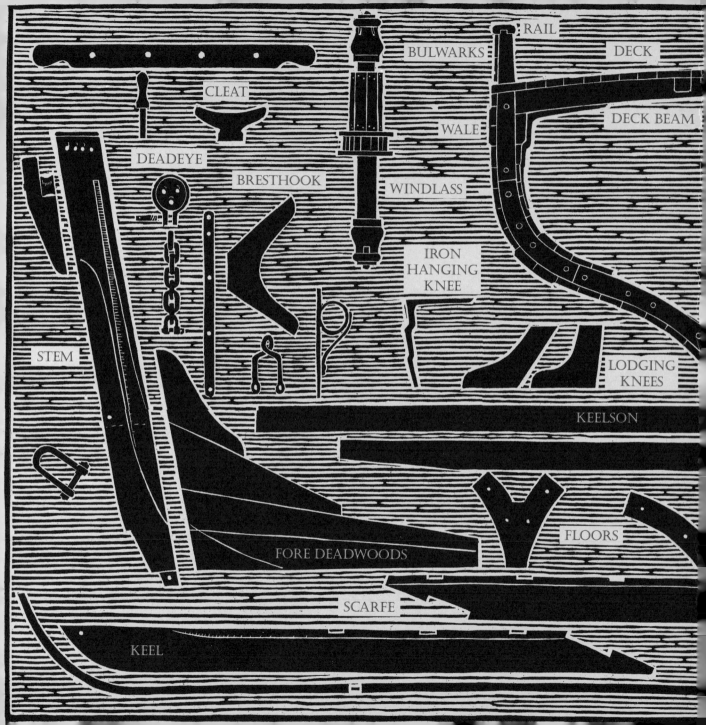